Various Ways to Explain ONE Thing

LOVE

In The
Present Tense

Mysteries Revealed

Anne Trippe

outskirts
press

Many Christians have been missing it.

The way we reign in Life and walk in freedom and power is a way we wouldn't expect - because it is a paradox to the natural human / world's way of thinking. It was a secret hidden since the beginning and for ages. It was a mystery.... until Christ revealed it. It is an image of God Himself.

And it is presented in this book,
LOVE in the Present Tense.

ENDORSEMENTS

Love in the Present Tense gives a comprehensive case for the centrality of love in Christian discipleship. Anne Trippe's excellent book is based on her respect for the whole counsel of God in Scripture and her clinical wisdom as a Biblical counselor. As our culture is being torn apart by reactionary hatred, God's people need to demonstrate His gracious love in their actions and reactions. But how? *This book gives a strong biblical, theological, and practical explanation* of how the believer can abide in Christ and be a vessel of God's love at home, at church, and in our turbulent world. This is an extremely important volume.

Dr. John Woodward
Grace Fellowship International

LOVE in the Present Tense is written *to believers who already know their new identity in Christ* and realize *this new identity is not simply for the purpose of having a better self-esteem* (not to diminish the profound impact that has). As people called to a new way of living that extends to others the love we have received from Christ, we wonder how to live out this higher calling.

Anne Trippe brings together scriptures that outline *the way of love* presented in the epistles. The *mysteries of Christ* beautifully unfold, *revealing the purpose of trials and suffering in a new light.* This book *reveals and teaches the new mindset* that we need in order to live out what God is working in us to bring us to maturity in Him.

Penny McAdams
Shepherd's Call Counseling

I'm so thankful for the way Anne lays the foundation for how the love of Christ gets expressed through us in tangible ways. She does such a great job in this book of unpacking the way Christ takes the new creation we've become at the spirit level and works through our souls and bodies to *live out who we've become in Him. This happens as we choose to renew our minds to the same attitude of Christ.* As we embrace what Anne teaches, we ourselves, our family, friends, and the unbelieving world around us will experience the outcome of Christ's Love being poured out through us.

Jason White,
Lead Pastor at Colonial Hills Baptist Church in Tyler, TX.

I read the book, **Love in the Present Tense** by Anne Trippe, and could not put it down. I worked with Anne Trippe in the Counseling Center at First Baptist Atlanta. She is a brilliant counselor. If you are willing to learn by reading and applying God's Truth to your life, **Love in the Present Tense** is for you. I encourage anyone who does not know how to love God's way to please read this book from cover to cover.

This book is for believers. Are you, as a believer, demonstrating God's unconditional love in all instances in your life, and toward everyone with whom you come in contact? Is the love you receive and then demonstrate God's *agape'* love? It is the answer. *My prayer is that people would hear the words and meaning of the scriptures that tell us about living out humility and the mind of Christ that is taught so beautifully in this book, in a language that is easy to understand, and apply these principles to their lives.*

If you know of anyone who is a believer - a friend, a son, or a daughter, or a couple that is going through hard times, this book would be the best gift you can give to that person.

Pastor Paul Diamond
Former Assistant to Pastor Emeritus Dr. Charles Stanley
First Baptist Atlanta

Anne does a brilliant job of sharing *the secret of God's love*. Books on God's love are a dime a dozen but Anne's book, **Love In The Present Tense**, is packed with the wisdom and truth that are in Christ. It points us back to the simplicity and purity of devotion to Christ as the only true source of experiencing God's transforming love and then living it out toward others - a mystery that was revealed by Christ. For those who open their heart to the treasure trove of wisdom and teaching in Anne's timely yet timeless book, be prepared to be challenged, inspired and encouraged by the endless love of the living God!

Bobby Allen, *Best-Selling Author of Relational Leadership and A Love Letter From God, Speaker, Life/Leadership/Emotional Intelligence/ Organization Coach and President of Legacy Leadership & Coaching*

There is no greater demonstration of love than the love God expressed to the world in the giving of His Son to die on the cross for our sins. However, God never intended His love to be an historical event, but an ongoing experience in the lives of all those who receive Jesus as their Savior, Lord, and Life. *Christ lives in us as our hope of glory, and that glory is **His love**, experienced by us, and expressed through us to others.* Thank you, Anne, for teaching us *what kind of LOVE that is,* and it is **Love in the Present Tense** to be lived in and through His church, so that the world will know that we are His disciples.

Frank Friedmann
Teaching Pastor, Grace Life Fellowship, Baton Rouge, LA

If you want to understand *God's ultimate intention* for every Christian, I urge you to read this excellent book by seasoned author, Anne Trippe. With much keen Biblical insight, she reveals the heart of God for every believer. At the end you may just say, "This is the kind of Christianity I've always wanted but never knew was possible."

Mark Maulding,
President of Grace Life International and Best-Selling Author of God's Best-Kept Secret

The mystery of God's Love is the main theme of Anne's new book, **Love In The Present Tense**. The mystery has been revealed in parables and through the Life and mind-set of Christ. God's unconditional Love is only possible by Christ as he manifests His love toward us and empowers believers by the Holy Spirit within them to give that Love to others.

Anne Trippe has been a well-known counselor and writer for many years. She has been one of my greatest Mentors. Her books have been so valuable in my own practice, as I have watched her words penetrate the ears and minds of many clients to help them find their righteousness, joy, and peace in Christ. The quest for love has put all of mankind "in a crisis" as they seek someone and/or something to fill those needs. Anne shows how receiving and then living out God's love is the answer.

Christine J Breen,
CMCP

In this book, Anne keeps coming back to our Father God's Word to show what we all need in life - to be loved by God. Then she **shares the mystery of how that love is to be lived out toward others**, and the answer can only be found in Jesus and *His mind-set of humility and being a servant*. In Him the way is found and is beyond what we could have ever imagined.

Ross Gilbert
Pastor of New Life Fellowship and Executive Director of Crossways to Life.

Table of Contents

Introduction

LOVE in the PRESENT TENSE - *Mysteries Revealed*

MANY **BELIEVERS IN Christ** are struggling in life and do not have any *lasting* peace nor joy. They often think their inner difficulties are because they or others aren't doing something right. Consequently, they condemn themselves, or others, and try by many strategies to avoid - or get past - any anxiety, emptiness, or feelings of rejection. And nothing works. They don't fully comprehend the reason for their struggles - nor the solution.

This book is written for the edification of those **born again believers who have received Jesus Christ as Lord and Savior**. For many of them, the answer to their inner conflicts has been elusive. They haven't heard that the solution was a *mystery* hidden in past ages but *now has been revealed* to believers through New Covenant truths.

The Greek word for *mystery* in the New Testament is not something we can't comprehend. But it is something that is revealed through the Word and by the Spirit.

In some scriptures, the word *mystery* refers to a symbol, an allegory or a parable, which may conceal its meaning from those who only hear it in a literal sense. Here a *mystery* is divine truth *once hidden, but now* **revealed or brought to light by the Gospel**. 2 Tim.1:10 And many expressions used to explain the truth of the Gospel can be *enig-mas* - or the opposite of - the world's definition of things.

The **mysteries** spoken of in this book are *GOD'S WILL* for us. Often people seek His will, thinking it only means an *outer doing* of a thing or being somewhere at a certain time. But we are about to **explore the MYSTERY of His will,** which in all wisdom and understanding **He MADE KNOWN to us** according to His good pleasure, which He purposed in Christ. Eph.1:8-9 NIV

After Jesus had been preaching the truth in parables to people, His disciples were wondering what the parables meant and asked Him about them. He replied, "To you has been given the **mystery** of the kingdom of God" (in parables). Mark 4:11 The **mystery** of the king-dom that was yet to come had been spoken in the parables. Parables were illustrations of *physical things* by metaphors that symbolize *spir-itual things*. But the people wouldn't be able to understand what the parables meant *until after His resurrection* when He would send the Holy Spirit to enlighten them.

Following Jesus' resurrection, the Apostle Paul was explaining the *mystery of Christ* to people when he said, "I do not want you to be **ignorant of this mystery**, brothers and sisters, *so that* you will not be conceited" *(So they wouldn't think they understood something when they really didn't)*. Rom. 11:25

Paul who was again sharing the gospel said, "the message I proclaim about Jesus Christ, is in keeping with **the revelation of the mystery hidden for long ages past,** but **now is revealed** and made known through the prophetic writings by the command of the eternal God, so that all the Gentiles might come to **the obedience that comes from faith**." Rom. 16:25-26

The ones who were spreading the good news about Christ to the people said, "we declare God's wisdom, a *mystery that has been hidden* and that God destined for our glory before time began." 1 Cor. 2:7 NIV

Paul also said, "If indeed you have heard of the administration of God's grace which was given to me for you, that by *revelation* it was made known to me *the mystery*, as I wrote before briefly. By referring to this, when you read you can understand my insight into the *mystery* of Christ." Eph.3:2-4 NIV

The **gospel is to enlighten** all people as to what the **plan** of **the mystery is,** which for ages had been *hidden in God*, who created all things; so that the multifaceted wisdom of God might **now** *be made known* Eph. 3:9-10

The mystery which had been *hidden from the past ages and generations*, but now **has been revealed** to His saints, to whom God willed to make known what the wealth of the glory of this **mystery** among the Gentiles, is *the mystery* that **is** *Christ in you,* the hope of glory. Col. 1:26-27

Yet again Paul said, "this **mystery is great**; but was speaking with reference to Christ and the church. Eph. 5:32   He also asked the church to *pray* in his behalf, that speech might be given to him to make known with boldness the **mystery of the gospel"**. Eph. 6:19

The mystery was revealed to people, so that their hearts would be encouraged, having been knit together in **Love,** and *that they would attain* to *all the* (spiritual) *wealth* that comes from the full assurance of understanding, *resulting* in a true **knowledge of God's mystery**, *that is,* **Christ** *Himself*, in whom are hidden all the treasures of wisdom and knowledge. Col. 2:2-3

Paul requested prayer that, "God will open up to us a door for the word, so that we may **proclaim the mystery** of Christ." Col. 4:3

It is called the **mystery of the faith** 1 Tim. 3:9 and the mystery of Godliness. Beyond question, **great** is the **mystery** of **Godliness.** 1 Tim. 3:16

> The truth of this MYSTERY that has now been revealed is something that seems absurd or contradictory to the natural world's way of thinking. But when it is experienced /explained, by the Spirit, proves to be true.

The truth has been revealed, and......

It is LOVE. In the Present Tense.

Various Words to Explain ONE Thing - LOVE.
That Mystery of Christ

There are many *words, metaphors, expressions* and *phrases* used in New Testament Scripture and in upcoming chapters in this book that are *different ways to* describe *various aspects* of the *SAME THING.* They are various ways of explaining ONE thing - *Faith being expressed through LOVE* - our sincere and pure devotion to Christ. 2 Cor. 11:3

The following are examples of those various words and phrases that communicate that *ONE* thing ...and *DO NOT* mean "DOING a lot of *DIFFERENT THINGS".*

For example:

Run the race	Humble	Lay aside	Press on
Set	Stand Firm	Obey	Fight
Labor	Persevere	Pursue	Walk
Cease	Prepare	Grow	Be transformed
Perfect	Be Conformed	Discipline	Take up
Serve	Arm yourself	Put on	Seek
Lay Hold	Enter in	Clothe	Mature
Possess	Know God	Renew	Abide

One of the biggest mysteries that is not explained here in this book is how God's Sovereignty and our will work together.

His ways are higher than our ways - beyond our human comprehension. But there are those things He has revealed and made known to the saints. Col. 1:25-27

CHAPTER 1

What IS LOVE - Anyway?

The words of the worship song

on Sunday were "I'm in rapture because of Your LOVE", and with hands lifted high they sang, "Your LOVE is wild, outrageous... I am taken away as I worship You." Their worship and love for God was being expressed at that time by emotions of exhilaration, being carried away with feelings of elation, jubilation or perhaps self-transcendence.

Well, if we don't have that definition of love, we usually think of LOVE as Affection. Connection. Attraction. A group of people were having lunch outside on a restaurant patio, when one said of her family, "They are so precious. I love them so much that I couldn't live without them." A man there was over-heard saying that he was falling in love and had never before been so attracted to a woman. In the same gathering, someone was telling how she loved a friend with whom she had bonded to the extent she felt they "knew each other's thoughts."

A song came to my mind. Romantic feelings emerged as the person sang something like this... "The kisses were magic...like butterflies and bubbling fountains. When I'm with you time stands still and I am filled....." Or something like that. And we thought that was love.

We use the word, *LOVE*, in different ways to describe how we *feel* about things. Our vacation. The flowers in the yard. Our job. The car we drive and so on. We can use it to refer to our various attachments. Many of us think of love only in terms of what we receive.

In this book, we are going to refer to LOVE as how it is defined and used in the New Testament. The ancient Greek language, in which the New Testament was written, had 2 main words for Love. The first is the noun, *agape* (the verb of which is, *agapao*). The second word is *phileo*.

- **Agape** – a noun, means God's VOLUNTARY, UNCONDITIONAL and SACRIFICIAL LOVE. *Agapao* is the verb form and means *action* motivated by that unconditional and sacrificial love. This kind of love is not inspired by emotion. It's expression is not forced nor manipulated. Rather, it is expressed by a determined choice.

  Agape is the Love with which God loves His Son and humans. John 3:16,35; 14:21; 15:19; 17:21-26 This love is God's will for His children regarding their attitude toward others. John 13:34, 1 Thess. 3:12 It expresses the **very nature of God**, 1 John 4:8 *Agape* love is known by the action it prompts. 1 John 4:9-10

- **Phileo** – means brotherly affection, friendship or emotions. It *can result* from *Agape* and may happen as a part of loving others with God's Love.

The Greek language also had terms for two other types of love, *Storge* and *Eros*. *Storge* means an empathy bond which is similar to *Phileo*. *Eros* means romantic love, sexual desire, physical attraction, and physical love. But these words DO NOT appear in the New Testament.

Most believers have heard that God LOVES us. But have we really let it sink in that:

- GOD Himself **IS** LOVE? 1 Jn. 4:8,16

That is HUGE especially when we know at the same time:

- God **IS** SPIRIT and
- He **IS** LIGHT. Jn. 4:24; 1 Jn. 1:5
- He **IS** ETERNAL LIFE. 1 Jn. 5:20

Because of that, the SPIRIT of God **IS** LOVE, and LOVE **IS** God's LIGHT, and **IS** God's POWER, and *IS* Eternal LIFE. God is not only the SOURCE of love, He *IS* LOVE. These INVISIBLE attributes *ARE* His Eternal LIFE and POWER. Rom 1:20 And THAT power created all things. Gen 1:1. Jesus was the **human image of the invisible God - of God's Power of LOVE, LIGHT and LIFE.** Jesus was the firstborn of all creation. Col. 1:15

For BY Him (BY **LOVE** - Spirit, Light, Life) ALL THINGS WERE CREATED in heaven and on earth, visible and invisible, whether thrones or dominions or rulers or authorities - all things were created THROUGH Him and FOR Him. And He IS before ALL things, and IN Him ALL things hold together. Col.1:16, Gen.1:1 He IS the beginning, and at the same time, the end. Rev. 21:6 Jesus Christ *is* the same yesterday and today and forever. Heb. 13:8 HE IS eternal LIFE. HE IS LOVE. So LOVE IS eternal LIFE. And it is LIGHT.

Christ is the POWER of God and the WISDOM of God. 1 Cor. 1:24; Acts 8:10 So LOVE is the POWER and WISDOM of **God**. Jesus said, "I am THE WAY and the TRUTH and THE LIFE. No one comes to the Father except through me. John 14:6 I and the Father ARE ONE." John 10:30 "In these last days (God) has spoken to us in His Son (Jesus), whom He appointed heir of all things, *through whom* also He made the world. And He (Jesus) is the radiance of His glory and the exact representation of His nature, and upholds all things by the word of His power." Heb. 2-3

"All things came into being through Jesus, and apart from Him nothing came into being that has come into being. In Him was LIFE, and the LIFE was the LIGHT of men. The LIGHT shines in the darkness, and the darkness did not comprehend it." John 1: 3-5 "This is the message we have heard from Him and announce to you, that God is LIGHT, and in him there is no darkness at all." 1 John 1:5

LOVE is the Spirit, Light, Life and Power that is ALL in ALL with no beginning and no end.

And Jesus, being God Jn. 10:30, *IS* LOVE = The Truth, The Way, The Life, The Light. Jn. 14:6, 8:12

THAT kind of LOVE is *Agapao*, and it is *all sufficient*. It is THE POWER of God.

God *IS* LOVE. LOVE *IS* God. LOVE IS God's Life and God's Light.

That kind of LOVE is healing, protection, provision, peace, rest, joy, righteousness. Love is PATIENT, love is KIND. It does NOT ENVY, it does NOT BOAST, it is NOT PROUD. It does NOT DISHONOR others, it is NOT SELF-SEEKING, it is NOT EASILY ANGERED, it keeps NO RECORD of WRONGS. Love does NOT DELIGHT in EVIL but REJOICES with THE TRUTH. It always PROTECTS, always TRUSTS, always HOPES, always PERSEVERES. **Love never fails.** 1 Cor. 13:4-8

Humans hunger for - **long for - LOVE,** but they may not realize it is *agape'* love that they long for.

That is LOVE in the Present Tense.

CHAPTER 2

Longing for Love?

For the most part, we have tried

to live life the best way we know how. And things may have gone well for a season. Then something happens. And we have struggled. Most of us have experienced loneliness, fear, rejection, guilt, shame, anger, depression, and emptiness at times. Some have found ways of trying to escape. And we have been inwardly tired of trying to measure up or find ways to feel LOVED - accepted, secure, fulfilled and at peace. And our trying hasn't worked.

We want all of those things....and what we probably want most is **to be loved.** Really. But many of us haven't understood what real love is, so we don't know how to **receive** OR **give** love. Some of us don't feel we are *worthy* of LOVE. Some of us are *afraid* of receiving LOVE. Some have been given a few accolades, enough material things, and maybe had some exciting – even romantic – times in life. Still...we don't understand why life isn't working. Or why we feel afraid, empty or sad, like we are missing something, like maybe *LIFE*.

The source of our struggles might be something we wouldn't suspect. To begin to comprehend it, we will journey back to the beginning to get a glimpse of how fear, emptiness and our own ways - our beliefs and behaviors for living life - develop and eventually turn out to be ineffective and even block the very things we long for. Although some of our ways might seem appealing...or even religious.

So. what's the problem?

As you know, in the beginning God created the first human in His likeness and image. He created him; male and female, He created them. Gen. 1:26, 27 He breathed His breath of LIFE into man. Genesis 2:7, 5:1 The Hebrew word for spirit is *ruach* - the same word for *breath* and *life* and *spirit*. The first humans had God's *LIFE in them*, and His Life was their SOURCE. (Remember that His *LIFE* **IS** LOVE, so LOVE was their source.) So they knew God and His LOVE and acceptance. They fellowshipped with Him, and their needs were met by Him.

BUT THEN, by Satan's *deception* one sinned, and eventually the other also sinned. God had previously told them if they disobeyed His one command to them, they would die. Gen. 2:17   Well of course they disobeyed, and as a result of their sin, **they died**. They did not die *physically* at that time, but *spiritually*. The word **'death' means separation.**

They were *SEPARATED* from experiencing God's *LIFE* – meaning His **LOVE - His peace, light, security, acceptance fulfillment** and **fellowship** with Him – **those same things *WE long for*!** And they were left with guilt and fear. They no longer experienced God's *LIFE* (His LOVE) dwelling in their human spirits! AND they were *bound by - slaves to* - the **power of sin**. Rom. 6: 6,16-17

Because of their sin, God set up things so the humans would even be *prevented* from going into another nearby garden and *partaking* of His *tree of LIFE*! Gen 3:24   They thirsted for God's LIFE, but may not have realized it was His LOVE and LIFE they were longing for.

That was a HUGE happening in the spiritual realm.

When their spirits had *died to - were **separated from** – knowing* God's *LIFE* – His *LOVE* and *POWER* - they were left depending only on their *human* spirit and mind and on their own resources. After their violation of God's command they were left empty, feeling condemned, needy, destitute and no longer complete. And they were **enslaved to the power of sin**! Rom. 6: 6,16-17

They were in a crisis.

The result was ***that all of mankind inherited their sin and death.*** Rom. 5:12,18 That means ALL are born "in Adam" – spiritually dead – **separated** from *knowing God – from experiencing His LOVE, His peace, His sufficiency,* and from being *empowered* by His *LIFE – His LOVE* in them . Eph. 2:1,4,5; 1 Cor.15:22; Rom. 3:23 And so from birth, all humans are born sinners – *bound by* sin. Rom. 6:6, 6:17

Therefore, just as through one human sin entered into the world, and death through sin, so death spread to all men, because all sinned. Rom. 5:12 Also through that ONE *transgression* there resulted *condemnation (and guilt)* to ALL! Rom. 5:18 All are **enslaved** by the **power of sin**!

*But we **might not know** we are bound by it, because sin can be deceptive and look either bad OR good OR even religious!* We might even think "sin" is just "lyin', cheatin', stealin', drinkin', and "runnin' round". BUT the word, **sin,** *means **"to miss the mark"*** - not live up to the attributes of God.

After Adam and Eve sinned (missed the mark), they were filled with inner pride, control, guilt, and fear. Because of their emptiness and neediness, they were driven to try to get from their performance and from each other, the things they had previously received so freely and unconditionally from God's LIFE – **His LOVE**. They walked independently of God as they tried to regain what had been lost – His LIFE - His *LIGHT, LOVE* and *SUFFICIENCY*. But they walked in darkness. Sin and death empowered them.

So it is with us - their descendants. *Since their sin, death, and neediness was inherited by all of us, and we were **bound and empowered by it**, we do just as they did.* We also draw conclusions and develop certain BELIEFS with our human understanding and according to the world's way of thinking about God and how to try to meet our needs, fill our longings, and rid ourselves of guilt. And find LOVE. But ineffective (perhaps even religious or attractive) behavior patterns are the result. These old beliefs and behaviors we develop are called "FLESH". And they are sin.

FLESH is all about *US*... our ways of trying to make life work for us ..and to find LOVE. And our ways *can seem* right! And PRIDE is involved. The word, *flesh*, almost literally means, "Trying to make life work the best way I know how". But walking after the FLESH is the *opposite* of LOVE - God's character of LOVE. And sooner or later, our fleshly ways for living life only bring frustration and emptiness, and any peace is elusive, temporary. We may feel as if we have failed and don't deserve LOVE.

And even though we may seek to know the one true God even by religious behaviors, we cannot, because we are *bound* by the *power* of *sin that dwells in us* and our *spiritual death* separates us from knowing God's Spiritual *LIFE – His light and Power – His LOVE*. It is with us just as it was with Adam and Eve... and their other descendants.

But THEN…Something happened.

Centuries after those first humans *missed the mark* and their sin and death was inherited by all of mankind, God gave HIS LAW to people. They thought if they successfully obeyed His Law that things would then go well with them. But guess what? It only *gave them KNOWLEDGE of their sin*! It REVEALED their sin. It brought their sin to their awareness! Rom. 3:20 The *Law* was good, but it actually only *EMPOWERED sin* in the people! 1 Cor. 15:56 Sinful passions are actually AROUSED by the Law! Rom. 7:5 And it brought about shame and a guilty conscience!

Back then religious LAW even included having animals to be sacrificed for the people's sin. It was a deeply symbolic ritual that only HID their sin for a while and then the sacrifices had to be done again… and again. The sacrifice was accepted as a temporary symbolic substitution for the lives of sinful people who were worthy of death.

But Old Testament sacrifices were not sufficient to pay for sin. In other words, they didn't atone for sin - which means they didn't reconcile or change – humans being separated from ***knowing* God**. The practice didn't work since they continued to try to live by the Law and it kept on *arousing sin* in them. They found no lasting inner peace, no joy nor fulfillment. The problem was that the LAW came to them so that their *transgressions (sin) would INCREASE*! Rom 5:18,20

And the animal sacrifices did NOTHING to FREE people FROM the *POWER OF SIN* IN them. It did nothing to bring back God's Spirit, His Life, Love, and Power TO DWELL IN people - His Life that He had placed in the first humans but was SEPARATED from them (and from all of us) when they sinned in the garden!

WHAAAT? Who knew?!

The **purpose** of His LAW was to show people how helpless they are as they try to live up to the Law's requirements in order to find God's LOVE, forgiveness, peace, joy, fulfillment and freedom from guilt by their own strength and resources. People can even focus on trying hard not to sin. But *it just doesn't work*. The sacrifices didn't take away sin. NOTHING is MADE PERFECT by religious law. It just REMINDS people of their sin! Heb. 10:1,3,11

Actually, the letter of the Law not only REVEALS sin, it KILLS! So, should it be a surprise that the Law was called, "The *LAW* of *SIN and DEATH*"? 2 Cor. 3:6, Rom. 8:2

When people try to live by their own personal fleshly rules/laws **OR** to live up to religious Law, instead of experiencing LOVE and any lasting peace the result was, and is, guilt, frustration, shame and often feeling rejected. We were bound by the *power of sin* that was in us**. And there was nothing we could do to deliver ourselves from that power,** *because* **we had been** *separated from God's LIFE and power***!**

Mankind was in a REAL crisis. They were prevented from knowing God's *agapao* LOVE – that LOVE which humans long for and need in order to experience LIFE, PEACE and JOY - and then to express that LOVE to others. It is the LOVE that we seek to find in people, places and things – but is not there. So we remain lonely, anxious, and often depressed.

All of that was a problem......actually **it still IS THE Problem...** *in the Present Tense*.

But a Solution was coming...

CHAPTER 3

The Solution.
In the Present Tense.

The fact is I've really

never enjoyed trying to solve problems. Math – that is. However, sometimes I do like to solve puzzles. The solution is often a MYSTERY. And the answer can be there in plain sight and I think, "Oh NO - how could I have missed it?"

But the solution to the crisis

that humans were in before *and* after God engraved His Law in stone wasn't so obvious. It was a real MYSTERY. The solution, in fact, had actually been *hidden* IN His Law! And there were clues in their religion with its animal sacrifices which were shadows - or symbols - of things to come - of the solution that would be revealed. Col. 2:17 It was a mystery and the people were missing it.

In God's timing and by His UNCONDITIONAL **LOVE**, MERCY and GRACE, He revealed the solution!

He sent His Son, Jesus Christ, to be the **one *sacrifice for sin for all time.*** Jesus did what the LAW and the SACRIFICES couldn't do. Jesus (who IS God) FULFILLED God's Law on our behalf! Jesus died to make the relationship between us and God RIGHT again! He **sacrificed Himself** for the sin by which we were bound so that we could be made RIGHTEOUS! He put an end to the death - our separation from God's LIFE - that we inherited. He ABOLISHED our spiritual DEATH! Matt. 5:17, Heb. 10:12, 2 Tim. 1:10 He ABOLISHED our SEPARATION from God's LOVE, LIFE and POWER!

It is *BY* religious LAW that *we learn we can't justify ourselves by our own efforts* or our WORKS of the LAW. It was *BY* Jesus' sacrifice that we were *justified*, which means simply *that we could be justified and **pardoned of our sins- forever**.* Jesus' sacrifice makes me **"*just as if I'd never sinned"***. And our being **justified** is only RECEIVED by FAITH in what the sacrifice of Jesus accomplished for us!

SO we BELIEVE in what He did in order to RECEIVE / experience our *justification* **by FAITH** and our *righteousness* in Him. It is NOT received by our WORKS of the Law; since by the works of the Law no flesh will be justified! Gal.2:16 Believers have been JUSTIFIED by Christ's DEATH! Rom. 3:24; 5:9,18; 6:6

So then as through *one transgression* (the first human's sin) there resulted *condemnation* to *all* humans, even so through *one act of righteousness* there resulted *justification of life* to *all* humans. For as through the **one** human's **disobedience** the many were **made sinners**, even so through the **obedience of** the **One** (Christ's death), the many will be **made RIGHTEOUS.** Rom. 5:17-19 *(If righteousness could be gained **through the law**, Christ died for nothing – in vain!)* Gal. 2:21

He made Him (Jesus) who knew no sin to **be sin** on our behalf, so that WE might *BECOME* the **RIGHTEOUSNESS** of **GOD** in Him. 2

Cor. 5:21 Our receiving this by faith does away with our condemning / shaming ourselves....because God doesn't condemn us. Rom. 8:1

To be **made** RIGHTEOUS means that *the righteousness of God* - which is His *Holiness* and *Purity* - was unconditionally given to humans by God. Believers by FAITH RECEIVE His righteousness and are made righteous in their SPIRIT. And It is called the *righteousness of faith*. Rom. 10:6; Phil. 3:9 The **SPIRITS** of *the* **righteous** are **made perfect.** Heb. 12:23

God has now *reconciled you in His body of flesh through death*, in order to present you before Him holy and blameless and beyond reproach. Col. 1:22 His *reconciling us* means that God **restored** our *original relationship with Him* so that we would **no longer be separated from Him and His LIFE**! And He did not do this according to our works, but *according to His own purpose and grace.* 2 Tim. 1:8-10

It was DONE. FINISHED. Now THAT is BIG!

We are told it is by GRACE that you have been saved (from sin and death) through FAITH; and THAT not of yourselves, *it is* the GIFT of God. Eph. 2:8 And having been *justified* by FAITH, we HAVE PEACE with God through our Lord Jesus Christ, and through Him we have obtained our introduction BY FAITH into this GRACE in which we stand. Rom. 5:2 So by exercising **faith** we can KNOW God - His character of LOVE, JOY, PEACE, healing and sufficiency in our mind, heart and soul instead of fear, and discouragement - not only in heaven after our bodies die, but as we live here **in this present world.**

Believers *receive* the *righteousness* of God through FAITH in Jesus Christ. Rom. 3:21 Phil. 3:9 It is only BY FAITH that **we believers** *are assured* that we are LOVED, *have been* JUSTIFIED and made RIGHTEOUS. Righteous means "being right" in the same way God is Right. We have been made *righteous!*

WOW.

God no longer holds any sin against believers for whom Christ died. We are *FORGIVEN* of ALL sin. Col. 2:13, Mark 3:28 Past, present and future sins. The one who by faith *believes*, RECEIVES that forgiveness *to enjoy here and now* and for eternity. Acts 10:43 Therefore, there is *now no condemnation* (no guilt) for those who are in Christ Jesus! Rom. 8:1

So let us draw near with a sincere heart in full *assurance of faith,* having *our hearts* sprinkled *clean from an evil conscience* (from guilt) and our bodies washed with pure water. Heb. 10:22 **God doesn't condemn us, and by faith we are to not condemn ourselves anymore!** We have been acquitted of guilt (declared not guilty) and brought into God's favor. IF we know and believe *by faith* we have been cleansed, **we no *longer have to live with a guilty conscience* (no condemnation) as we live in our mortal bodies!**

Another HUGE thing!

Well. Since all of that is God's incomprehensible gift to us by His GRACE, just **what *IS* GRACE? God's grace** is the English translation of the Greek χάρις (charis) meaning, *gifts which bring delight, joy, happiness*. The word, GRACE, represents *all God IS for us and to us*. By His grace we will never be condemned nor punished for our sins Rom. 8:1 (We must know that being *convicted* of sin and being *condemned* because of sin are two different things.)

God Himself took on flesh and blood and became human like we are, so that through His physical death He would **render powerless him who had the power of death, that is,** the *devil,* and might **free those** who were subject to slavery all their lives by their fear of death. Heb. 2:14-15

The *LAW of the Spirit of LIFE* in Christ Jesus has **SET YOU FREE** from the **LAW of sin and of death!** Rom. 8:2 He also *made us **adequate as servants*** of a New Covenant, NOT of the LETTER (of religious law) but of the SPIRIT; for the letter (the Law) KILLS, but the SPIRIT gives LIFE. 2 Cor. 3:6

And who knew this...the **Law** makes ***nothing* perfect!** Heb. 7:19 Even more, the sting of death is sin, and the POWER of SIN is the LAW; but thanks be to God, who gives us the victory (freedom from the Law) through our Lord Jesus Christ. 1 Cor. 15:56-57 Wow. We are NO LONGER BOUND by the power of sin and death! Jesus abolished death - our separation from God's Life and Spirit 2 Tim. 1:10, so that we might be **joined as one** spirit **with the Lord.** 1 Cor. 6:17

But now we have been RELEASED FROM the LAW, having **died to** (been separated from) that (power) by which we WERE BOUND, *so that we can serve in newness of the Spirit* and NOT in oldness of the letter (of religious LAW) as we live and relate in this world. Rom. 7:6

Jesus didn't do away with God's Law, He fulfilled it on our behalf. He said, "Do not think that I came to abolish the Law or the Prophets; I did not come to abolish but to FULFILL it". Matt. 5:17 It was ONLY because of God's GRACE and unconditional LOVE for us that He **fulfilled His law** and **abolished the power of death** for us so we can have fellowship with Him and **partake of His LIFE, LOVE, POWER, protection, healing, joy** and **sufficiency** as we *live daily in this life,* as well as *in the life to come.*

So we are not to call to mind the former things or consider things of the past. God said in prophecy, "Behold, I am going to do something NEW. Now it will spring up; Will you not be aware of it? I will even make a roadway in the wilderness, Rivers in the desert" Isa. 43:18-19. And He DID IT. He fulfilled the Prophecy.

HE has done it ALL. God's work on our behalf is FINISHED. He MADE us right with Him. We are forever secure in Him. John 14:16 Being **justified by His grace** we would be made heirs according to *the* hope of Eternal Life. Titus 3:7

We may not FEEL all of this is true as we walk through hard times, un-fairness, loss and disappointments of daily life. So we need **to know the Truth** that **sets us free.** John 8:32 FREE from the power of guilt from our past, free from anxiety and from the power our fleshly be-liefs and resulting behaviors have had over us. We must RECEIVE the Truth. By faith.

That is the *amazing* truth of God's UNCONDITIONAL LOVE and GRACE - in the Present Tense. So how does this all apply to me as I live in this world and relationships?

Well **it was a MYSTERY** that **HAS BEEN REVEALED.**

That is LOVE in the Present Tense.

CHAPTER 4

Mysteries Revealed

I have always been intrigued

by **MYSTERIES**. Even when I was a child I was glued to the Nancy Dew Mystery books as well as others that pursued and uncovered the seemingly unexplainable. Have you ever been captivated by Mysteries?

Had you even been aware there are references to **MYSTERIES** in New Covenant scripture? The word, *MYSTERY*, in Scripture can refer to sacred secrets – things that had been hidden in the past but were eventually revealed or "brought to light".

In the Word of God, a MYSTERY can be something that evades human understanding, or when something is a paradox; two truths that are seemingly contradictory. Humanly speaking we can be intrigued by mysteries. Among the places in the New Testament where the "mystery of the gospel" is referenced are in Rom. 6:25, and Eph. 3:6; 6:19.

The truths that have been addressed here in former chapters are really *mysteries to* our own human reason. The truths of God's unconditional LOVE for us and our being forgiven and set free from the power of sin and death is a mystery. Another MYSTERY is that our being *separated* from God's Spirit and from being able to *KNOW* HIM, His Love and Peace *was abolished* because believers are now JOINED as ONE SPIRIT with Christ.

That means believers who were DEAD in sin are made ALIVE spiritually (born again) by His (eternal) LIFE in us and declared righteous before God. Rom. 6:11, 1 Cor. 15:22; Eph. 2:4-5 The good news of the New Testament is to REVEAL those SECRETS - those truths - to those who have been born of His spirit. The *gospel* is to bring a believer's LIFE and IMMORTALITY to light – to reveal it to them! 2 Tim.1:10

But did YOU KNOW that?!
What *AMAZING LOVE* is THAT!

The first humans had God's LIFE *WITHIN* them, but then they were separated from knowing that LIFE. But by God's love, mercy and grace, He gave His LIFE, LOVE and POWER to INDWELL humans! And this time, Believers are *made aware by the gospel* that His LIFE will live forever in them. 2 John 1:2. They have been JOINED WITH THE LORD and **one spirit with Him**. 1 Cor. 6:17 And nothing can again separate them from the LOVE of God. Rom. 8:35-39 The Love of God lives in our new spirit.

We, who by FAITH believe and receive the truth, have been born a second time – **BORN OF THE SPIRIT.** John. 3:5-8 It is a spiritual birth, where God imparts His Life / Spirit to literally indwell our new spirit. We are accepted in Him, NEW CREATIONS with a new nature and new identity. Since our spirit is our basic nature, *spiritually* we become HOLY, SAINTS, and the very RIGHTEOUSNESS of God in Christ, Rom. 3:22, Eph. 1:4, 2:19, 4:12 **Now THAT is a *Mystery*!**

We are literally placed in union with Christ, which is the **MYSTERY** *that was hidden* in past ages, but NOW is REVEALED to the saints. It is the **MYSTERY** of **Christ in us**, our hope of glory. It is **the MYSTERY** which for ages had been hidden in God who created all things. Col. 1:26-27, Eph. 3:9   Jesus said, "In that day you will KNOW that I am in My Father, and you in Me, and **I in you**." John 14:20, 17:21

Believers are joined with Christ and in Him all the fullness of Deity dwells in bodily form, and in Him *you have been made (spiritually)* **complete**, and He is the head over every ruler and authority.   Col: 2:10   This means that according to His divine power, He has *given unto us all things that pertain unto life and godliness, through the knowledge of Him* that hath called us to glory and virtue" 2 Peter 1:3 Yes, It's true, even though we may not have *experienced* or laid hold on it all yet *in our human mind and emotions.*

Nothing can separate us from His **love** - neither death, nor life, nor angels, nor principalities, nor things present, nor things to come, nor powers, nor height, nor depth, nor any other created thing, will be able to *separate* us (ever again) from the love of God, which is in Christ Jesus our Lord. Rom. 8:35-39

Our being joined with Christ is one of *the MYSTERIES of the Kingdom of God.* Luke 8:10

But now... did you know this.... ANOTHER MYSTERY

Our *old self* was actually **crucified with** *Christ* in the spiritual realm, so that our body of sin (the **power** *of sin* in us) might be **done away with**, so we would **no longer be slaves** to sin. Rom. 6:6   It was so sin would no longer have power over us.   The **power of sin IS** the old religious **LAW**. 1 Cor. 15:56   And the law of the Spirit of life in Christ Jesus has set you **free from** the **LAW of sin and of death**. Rom. 8:2

Our *old self was* CRUCIFIED *with* Christ, therefore if anyone is *in Christ, he* **is a new creature**; the *old things passed away*; behold,

NEW things have come. 2 Cor. 5:17-18 It is that NEW thing which was prophesied in Isaiah.

For **you have died** and your *life is hidden with* **Christ in** *God*. Col. 3:3 I am *crucified with* Christ: nevertheless I live; yet not I, but *Christ* **lives in me**: and the life which I now live in the flesh (body) I live by the faith of the Son of God, who loved me, and gave Himself for me. Gal. 2:20 (KJV) And the REASON for all of this is that, **just as** Christ was raised from the dead through the glory of the Father, so **we also may walk in newness of life.** Rom. 6:4

Whoever believes in the Son HAS eternal LIFE, but whoever rejects the Son will not see LIFE, for God's wrath remains on them. John 3:36 So by FAITH, we who believe the Truth, are to *consider ourselves* to be *dead to sin*, but ALIVE *to* God in Christ Jesus. Rom. 6:11 Regardless of how we feel emotionally…Wow, a HUMONGUS truth!

Regarding becoming a NEW creature with new LIFE in Christ. Jesus said, "Do not be amazed that I said to you, 'You must be **born again.'** "Truly, truly, I say to you, unless one is *born again* he cannot see the kingdom of God." That which is born of the flesh is flesh, and **that which is born of the Spirit is spirit.** Jn. 3: 3,5-6,7 Born again people become the *temple* of God. 1 Corinthians 3:16; 6:19. We are literally placed in Christ and He in us. Being in Christ, we have also been placed with Him in the Father. 1 Cor. 1:30, John 14:20

Again, we see that believers *have* God's ETERNAL LIFE / SPIRIT / POWER dwelling *in their NEW* **SPIRIT**. Blessed be the God and Father of our Lord Jesus Christ, who according to His great mercy has caused us to be BORN AGAIN to a living hope through the resurrection of Jesus Christ from the dead. 1 Peter 1:3 Eternal life is more than never ending life. It is a QUALITY of life that is our living joyfully, without condemnation from God, and at peace. We have been equipped to walk in NEW Life and Power!

Sometimes we hear believers speak of having a *new HEART*. In the New Testament, the words *spirit* and *heart* might be used a few times as overlapping or interchangeable. But the word, HEART, **usually** refers to one's SOUL or MIND as it is the location of our *human* mind - thoughts, decisions, and emotions, which wasn't made new when we were born again in our spirit. It is *by the Power of His Spirit* infused into our new spirit that we believe the truth in our human MIND/heart.

We are SPIRIT beings, and believers have been made NEW in spirit – NEW CREATIONS. Believers *receive* His Spirit, His Power, Peace, Forgiveness, and Righteousness - by "hearing with faith" Gal. 3:2. Faith comes forth and is *activated* by hearing the Word of God. Rom. 10:17. Remember, He brings our LIFE and IMMORTALITY to light (reveals it) by the gospel. 2 Tim. 1:10

> When Believers are born of God's Spirit, we are *born free* from the chains of sin, death and condemnation that *enslaved* us. And we have His Life and Power - Christ's Life / the Holy Spirit - indwelling our new SPIRIT in exchange for the sin and death that empowered us and separated us from Him. HE became our NEW LIFE. Col. 3:4   HE is LOVE, and LOVE is our new POWER for living and LOVING others that now indwells us.

Yes, again you might be thinking you sure don't FEEL as if all of this is true. Before we can experience for ourselves and express to others God's Eternal LIFE, LIGHT and LOVE, we must first, by faith, RECEIVE God's LOVE. We, as NEW CREATIONS, must receive what we HAVE and WHO we ARE – and **know** that Christ in us is our new *power*, our *sufficiency* and our *adequacy*.

We have *thought we had to live up to certain standards* to find our identity, to feel loved and accepted, and to be emotionally healed.

21

But now we believers can *know* we have a *new identity* within, a *new power* to live Life differently and *be free* from the heavy weights we carried - from the chains that bound our hearts and minds.

In the past, we have seen ourselves as a result of what we do, what material THINGS we have, and what others THINK of us and so on... But as believers, we must begin to think differently about WHO we ARE and Christ's LOVE, provision and protection that resides in us.

So WHO do you *think* you are – and why?

That is LOVE in the Present Tense.

CHAPTER 5

So.... *Who* Do You Think You Are?

Most of us believe

that what HAPPENS TO us in this world gives us **our identity** - makes us **who we are**. Or we believe what we DO can make us **who we are,** or what we HAVE, where we LIVE, or our ACCOMPLISHMENTS make us **who we are**. Or what OTHERS THINK makes us **who we are,** or we must be TREATED FAIRLY to verify **who we are**. Well, and for some of us if our TEAM WINS it certifies **who we are**. Many **believe** we must BE IN CONTROL and/or BE RIGHT to attest to **who we are**. We try hard to establish our **worth**, fill our emptiness and drive away our loneliness in many ways such as work, fun, excitement, relation- ships - or perhaps even substance abuse.

We can **think** many of these pursuits give us *our identity* or make us more *acceptable*. And we go after those things by many different means. We often try hard. But for some reason any identity or signifi- cance we find by our strategies doesn't satisfy us for long and they do not make us feel *of value, secure, content,* or *loved.* ***Sometimes our strategies look good and seem right***.... but they eventually backfire on us.

And we wonder why our ways haven't worked. It is because these beliefs and our resulting behaviors *do not make us WHO we are*.

Well then, what *does* make us WHO are we?

Many believers haven't heard that they have *literally* been born again, becoming new creations in Christ. When believers are born again – born of God – we are given a *new spirit*, joined as one with Christ in our SPIRIT. 1 Cor. 6:17 Because of this, we have a NEW IDENTITY. And sin no longer has any power over us. When we hear that, we might be confused and wonder why we still sin and often feel defeated in life if that is true.

As born-again believers, we all deal with difficulties in our daily lives and relationships. In our HUMAN MIND, we as believers can still think as we always thought about what is necessary for us *to be who we are*; and for us to feel accepted, secure, of worth, and at peace. We can still make decisions and respond the way we have always done. We can wind up feeling disappointed, tired, depressed, fearful, angry or even unforgiving. So there is often confusion and misunderstanding regarding why we can't seem to rise above our circumstances and emotions. The answer is that we need to awaken to who we are in Christ and to what He has provided for us.

To explain, it first might be helpful to describe **the spiritual and physical make-up of humans.**

Humans are made up of three parts: SPIRIT, SOUL *and* BODY. 1 Thess. 5:23 The SPIRIT is the **EMPOWERING** force in us and our basic nature or identity. Humans ARE SPIRIT beings. *Our spirit determines who we are.* It is our identity.

Then we HAVE a SOUL, or *psyche'*, area which is made up of one's human MIND, will and EMOTIONS. When scripture speaks of our 'heart', it is *usually* referring to our SOUL – our *mind - our beliefs or attitudes*. **Our SOUL area is not automatically transformed when we are born again; only our spirit is changed and empowered**. And we live in the third part of our being - a BODY.

Our **beliefs** and **the resulting emotions** and **behavior patterns** which were formed in our human mind / **SOUL** by the *world system* in which we live and by the *power of sin*, are referred to as **FLESH**. They are patterns that may *look bad OR may look good and even seem religious*. They are familiar ways to us. But these are the *ineffective* ways we have developed in an effort to make life work for us according to our own human understanding. These beliefs and attitudes are lived out through the third part of our being which is our BODY.

We usually think that our FLESH patterns represent who we are – our identity. The truth is, **they do NOT represent who we are as new creations in Christ.** When we live by these old *fleshly beliefs* and the resulting behaviors, even though they may *seem* right, they only defeat us. And they BLOCK our experience of all that is ALREADY ours in Christ.

> Born again humans are *empowered* by a new **SPIRIT** (Christ in us) *so that* we can CHANGE OUR old former BELIEFS and be *transformed in our* **SOUL** by RENEWING our HUMAN MIND to the likeness of Christ who indwells our **SPIRIT**! Rom. 12:2

How many believers have heard that?

Believers were given this encouragement: May the God of peace Himself *sanctify* you **entirely**; and may your **spirit** and **soul** and

body be preserved complete, without blame at the coming of our Lord Jesus Christ. We, as **new creations**, *have actually been* made perfect, holy, sanctified, complete **in our SPIRIT** and have been *equipped* there with everything that pertains Life and Godliness. 2 Peter 1:3

In order **to experience** what we *already have* - God's Life and His Godliness - that dwells in our SPIRIT- and **to BE** who we *already ARE* in Christ and enjoy that victorious LIFE - we must be *TRANSFORMED* in our HUMAN MIND (in our SOUL) - to that SAME MIND-SET of Christ that resides in our SPIRIT and let it be lived out through our BODY.

This transformation is a growing and maturing process. *As we are being transformed by the renewing of our mind*, we begin to *experience* in our SOUL our sanctification in Christ. We *experience* the peace, fulfillment, joy and clear conscience that is ALREADY ours. **We begin to *experience* what is already true spiritually.** This happens *when we are being transformed and conformed to Christ's attitude / likeness.* It is also when we KNOW HIM more fully. These concepts will be explained more in future chapters of this book.

To be *sanctified* means to be *set apart* because we belong to Him. We *have been* **sanctified** through the offering of the body of Jesus Christ *once for all.* For by one offering He has perfected for all time those who are sanctified. Heb. 10:10,14. **In the spiritual realm we believers *have been* sanctified and perfected in *all 3 aspects* of our being,** spirit, soul and body. The spirit is sanctified when we are born again. The soul (mind, will and emotions) is in the process of *appropriating* our sanctification, and the body will eventually be set apart from its sin and mortality at our resurrection. (Eph. 4:24;1 Pet. 1:14-16; Phil 3:20,21).

Our SPIRIT *has been made alive and sanctified because we are joined as one spirit with Christ.* But the *reason* we are to *be in the process* of being **TRANSFORMED** in our SOUL (mind) to His likeness that is in our SPIRIT, *is so that His LOVE, LIFE, PEACE and sufficiency might be known and experienced by us and through us - instead of the pride, emptiness, incompetence, fear and guilt we often feel and convey while living life by our old FLESHLY beliefs that reside in our SOUL.* As we are being transformed, our old *strategies that **block*** our experience of God's peace, joy and righteousness, are gradually left behind.

SO just HOW are we to BE TRANSFORMED by the RENEWING of our Human MIND? First, we are to change our mind and SET IT ON the TRUTH of God's LOVE, protection, and provision for us, on who He is in us, on who we are in Him, and on His mind-set. This process will be explained more in future chapters.

That is LOVE in The Present Tense

Following are illustrations to help visualize who we are as humans and how these truths apply.

A Biblical Picture of Humans:

Mankind: A Three-Part Whole. I Thessalonians 5:23, Hebrews 4:12

Body, Soul & Spirit

This illustration depicts a person *IN* Adam *walking IN* the Flesh
Romans. 8:8

The **gray areas** depict the sin and spiritual death / separation from God in a person before she/he is born-again. The POWER OF SIN drives this person, as she/he lives in his/her environment, to draw conclusions (False Beliefs) about God, self, and how needs are to be met, which are stored in the SOUL and lived out through the BODY. The resulting outer actions can look good OR bad. **Spiritual death separates this person from knowing God.** One's identity is SINNER. Rom. 5:8

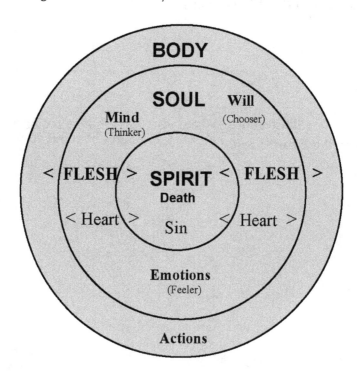

In the Greek, **the word "heart"** is from the word, _kardia_, which means the physical organ, OR it means "the seat of emotions ", "inclinations", "desires," "purposes", or "mind". In the Hebrew mindset, the "heart" was the seat of one's personality and reason and thoughts. (There seems to be only a few times where the word "heart" can be used interchangeably for mind or spirit).

The word **psyche** _(ψυχὴν)_ can be a problem for translators when they translate Christ's words, because they can translate them to mean two different things: a person's "soul" and his "life." In the NT, it is translated 58 times as "soul," 40 times as "life," and three times as "mind".

A New Creation In Christ

This person is *In* **the Spirit** - but **walking** *After* **the Flesh** Rom. 8:9

This shows a person whose spirit of sin and death has been replaced with Christ's Spirit and Life. This person has been born again of the Spirit. **Christ is now the person's identity, sufficiency and power. However, the person is not yet walking according to the Spirit, but according to the flesh.** The old fleshly patterns in the MIND *block* the person and others from experiencing Christ's life in and through him/her.

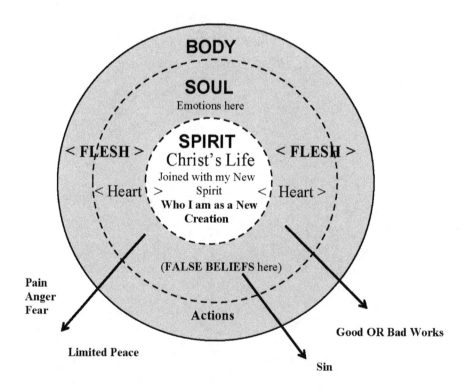

The solution is that this Believer would be **Transformed by the Renewing of his/her Human Mind to the same Mind-set of Christ that**

dwells in his/her spirit. Rom. 12:12 We must have a change of mind from our Old beliefs to Truth so we can walk in and more fully experience Who Christ is in us and who we are in Him, so others might see Him through us.

CHAPTER 6

Well Then... Let's Change Our Minds

And Be Transformed

In *The Sacred Romance*, Curtis and Eldridge tell us, "We anesthe-tize our hearts from feeling their emptiness by competence or order of some kind, with redemptive busyness, or by some form of indul-gence. And to free ourselves by will power or external discipline is futile. The only power is in the attitude of our internal being – the choice of our heart." (p. 154).

A scholarly definition of **FLESH** is that the word represents trust in one's *(human)* self as being able to procure life through one's own *(human)* strength, and accomplishments. Both *(religious)* legalism and lawlessness are fleshly in so far as they both hold out a false promise of (a supreme quality of) life on the basis of man's efforts."

> * From the *New International Dictionary of New Testament Theology*, Vol. 1, pp. 680, 681.

The Word tells those of us who have become new creations, that ALL OF OUR needs for an abundant life ARE SUPPLIED IN CHRIST.

But this may not be our *experience*. However, because of our new birth, we have been empowered by God's Spirit to be able to choose to focus on Truth and CHANGE our FALSE MIND-SET about WHO WE ARE, how our NEEDS are MET and how to KNOW CHRIST who indwells us. As a result of this change of MIND, our *old ineffective* FLESH patterns of trying to meet our needs and find what we long for will be *gradually - abandoned*.

Scripture refers to this change as ***being transformed*** *by the* ***renewing of our mind***. Rom. 12:2 The word, *repentance,* in New Testament Greek is *metanoia* and literally means "a turning around by a change of MIND", and it means the RENEWING of OUR human MIND. It also has the meaning of a change of the will regarding sin and the obedience of faith. Acts 20:21; 26:20

Our thinking and attitudes determine our emotions and behaviors.

Renewing of the mind results in one being TRANSFORMED. Our transformation does not happen by outer "behavior modification". It is learning to *walk* ***by / according to the mind-set of Christ's SPIRIT*** *within us rather than according to our FLESHLY beliefs and the resulting defeating emotions and behaviors*. By this, Christ's Life, Sufficiency, Joy, and Peace will be ***experienced*** by us and ***lived out*** through us.

It is for our good and God's glory that we are given this exhortation: "And do not be conformed to this world, but be **transformed** by the **renewing** of your **mind**, so that you may ***prove what the will of God is, that which is good and acceptable and perfect.*** Rom.12:2

God's love, patience and kindness, plus our *Godly* sorrow that is according to His will, lead us to our ***repentance.*** These things lead us to turn around by a CHANGE of our MIND. And it involves our desire to be Godly, while worldly or fleshly sorrow only leads to death (our being separated from knowing God's peace and love). Rom. 2:4; 2 Cor. 7:6-10

As a new creation in Christ, our *being transformed and healed inwardly* means we put off (in our thinking) our old self which is being corrupted by its deceitful desires; to be **made NEW in the attitude of OUR MIND**; and **to put on** (in our mind/thinking) **the new self,** (which has ALREADY been) **created like God in true righteousness and holiness**. Eph. 4:22-24 NIV

We WERE made NEW in our SPIRIT, and NOW we are **to be** MADE NEW in the attitude of our MIND – with our MIND being CONFORMED to the same attitude of Christ that dwells in our Spirit. We **do *not*** do this by *focusing* on "putting off the old self". The "**old self" or our old thinking and mind-set** is *put off or abandoned* as we focus on putting on **the NEW in our thinking**.

Since then, you have been raised with Christ, SET your MIND (*heart* - NIV) on things above, where Christ is seated at the right hand of God. SET your MIND on things above, not on earthly things. Col. 3:1-2 NIV (This refers to Truths that are higher than earthly ways of thinking.) For the MIND set on the flesh is *death*, but the MIND set on the Spirit is LIFE and PEACE. Rom. 8:6 So **let** this **mind be in you** that is **also in Christ.** Phil. 2:5-8 The attributes of the Spirit - the mind of Christ - are "the things above" spoken of here.

Yes. Our *old self was crucified with Christ, and we are already new creations in our **Spirit**. But our **old ways and thinking which are left over from our old self** still remain in the attitude of our **human mind – our Soul.** And these old ways will be abandoned (put off) as we focus on renewing of our human mind to the mind-set of Christ. In that particular scripture, Eph. 4:22-24, the "old self" refers to the fleshly attitude of our human mind-set and does not describe WHO we are as new creations in Christ.

So what DO You Believe?

The source of our fears and struggles could be something that we might not suspect. It can be helpful to explore how our belief system – our thinking – might be involved in these dilemmas. Once we are born again, we *can* continue to think according to our "pre-salvation" state. We think like we've always thought. We respond to people like we've always responded. And we think of ourselves as we've always thought of ourselves.

It's time for a **new way** of thinking: a *belief system that reflects our new nature and the Truth that is contained in Scripture about who God is in us and for us and what He has given us.* We need to "re-train" our mind (our heart). We frequently are not aware that we are thinking wrongly. Our old beliefs *can* often seem so right and accept-able that we don't realize they are **keeping us defeated**.

But they *can be the "terrorists" in our lives and be at the root of our fears and the devastating emotions in our Soul.* Janet Newberry said, "Our habits of relating and communicating today are often rooted in the lies we believed a long time ago." Even as children, we began forming *our own* **lies** - **our own** laws to live by, becoming a law unto ourselves, and then as a result, condemning ourselves (or others)!

So it can be helpful to begin to identify some of our incorrect ways of thinking. When renewing our mind to truth, especially in the begin-ning, we might not *feel* or experience the truth and our new LIFE in Christ right away.

It takes time and is a process of learning to exercise faith. We must learn to **set our mind on things above** (on the Truth) and NOT on the ways the world system reasons about how fulfillment, security and peace are to be found. And we are to do this BECAUSE "you have died and your (new) LIFE is HIDDEN with Christ in God." Col. 3:3

Again, those "things above" are on the *heavenly* things – the TRUTHS of a different realm.

We must trust that God's Spirit within us *is* Truth and *is* LOVE - and *is* our healer, provider, protection and power. When we choose to renew our thinking to these truths regardless of how we might feel, we will begin to experience healing of damaged emotions, and doubt and fear will be left behind.

My friend, Christine, said it well when she stated, "Our SPIRIT person is saturated with God's Life. Our SOULS are the part BEING TRANSFORMED by the renewing of our minds SO WE CAN LIVE the VICTORIOUS LIFE that Paul wrote about. We have been given the power to replace the lies with truth, and walk as children of light. Then, when we get to heaven we'll discover all we never learned. The mysteries will ALL be revealed!

Those heavenly things we are to think on are whatever is **true**, whatever is **honorable**, whatever is **right**, whatever is **pure**, whatever is **lovely**, whatever is **commendable**, if there is any **excellence** and if anything **worthy of praise**, think about these things. Phil. 4:8 (And we are not to set our focus on those things according to how the world interprets them). But HOW do we DO that?

The answer will be explained in future chapters. As we, by His Power in us continue in faith, His Life will be **experienced by** us and be **revealed through us** for others to see. Col. 3:4

Following is a table presenting **False Beliefs vs Truth**. It is a table of typical wrong beliefs about how we expect needs and longings to be met in life. They are contrasted with Scriptural Truth so you might begin to set your mind on Truth – on "things above". As you read through the chart, consider marking the False Beliefs that pertain to you and compare each with the Truth.

Some Examples of False Beliefs vs Truth

You may use the following table to identify some of your False Beliefs about how longings and needs of Security, Worth and Peace are to be met. It may help you to be aware of any unconscious beliefs you have. Focus on replacing them with truth.

A more extensive table can be found in my book, *Old Beliefs vs New Beliefs*.

False Beliefs   vs   Truth

False Beliefs	Truth
1. I must control my circumstances for me (and my family) to be **secure.**	I am secure because I am hidden with Christ in God. Col.3:3. All my needs are supplied in Christ. Phil. 4: 19 It is not by my power nor strength, but by His Spirit. Zech.4:6 He is a shield to those who walk uprightly. Pr. 2:7b
2. I must perform perfectly and avoid mistakes to be **acceptable.**	I am perfect in Christ; one spirit with Him. Heb.10:14; I Cor. 6:17 I have been made accepted by Him. Eph.1:6 Christ died that I would be the righteousness of God in Him. 1 Cor. 5:21

3. I must stay emotionally guarded to be safe and **secure.**	The Lord is my safety. Ps. 4:8; 27:1-6; 32: 7-11 Safety is only of the Lord. Pr. 1:33; 3:23; 21:31 As I trust Christ, His peace will guard my heart and mind. Phil.4:7 He is my shield and fortress. Ps. 18:1-3 But the Lord is faithful, and he will strengthen you and protect you from the evil one. 2 Thess. 3:3
4. I must be strong and independent to **survive.**	Christ's strength is perfect in my weakness. II Cor.12: 9 My life is to be dependent on Christ, since He is the Vine and I am a branch in Him. Without Him I can do nothing. John 15:5; II Cor.12:10
5. I am entitled to get respect from, and be appreciated by others to know I am **of worth** and not rejected.	Christ has made me accepted and perfect. Eph.1: 6; Heb.10:14 See #2 I am called to love, and to serve others and consider them better than myself. Phil. 2:3 Pride comes before destruction and shame. Pr.16:18; 11:2 I am to become of "no reputation" and be a servant. Phil. 2:5-8.

6. I need others to accept me and treat me fairly so I can find **peace.**	Jesus Christ is my peace and gives me peace. John 14:27 I am in perfect peace when my mind is fixed on Him. As I humble myself, I will enjoy the peace He has given me. Ps. 37:11, Is. 26:3
7. What I do makes me **who I am.**	Birth determines my identity. I have been made a new creation by my new birth. The old me died with Christ. Gal. 2: 20; II Cor. 5: 17
8. I am **inadequate.** I must please others to know I am **acceptable.**	I have been made adequate. 2 Cor.3:5-6 I can do all things through Christ. I am complete in Him. Col.2:10; Phil.4:13 He makes me adequate to do His will. Heb.13:21 See #9
9. I must prove I am right to know I am **of worth**.	Christ has made me accepted in Him. Eph.1: 6; Ps.139, 13-18 I am chosen, righteous, holy, a saint: A new creation. II Cor.5:17; I Peter 2: 9; I Cor.1: 2; 5:21 See #2, #5

10. People from my past must change (admit their offenses against me, etc.) before I can be free of my childhood issues and **be O.K**	My issues *have* been dealt with because I have spiritually died with Christ and am born a new creation with power to walk in newness of life. Rom. 6:4 I can be O.K. when I accept that He has given me the victory. I can cease from my struggling. Heb.4:10

Some scriptures defining who you are in your spirit person - as a new creation in Christ

John 1:12	A child of God - part of His family. Rom. 8:14-16
John 15:1-5	Part of the true vine, a channel (branch) of His (Christ's) life.
John 15:15	Christ's friend.
John 15:16	Chosen and appointed by Christ to bear *His* fruit.
Rom. 8:17	A joint-heir with Christ, sharing His inheritance with Him.
I Cor. 3:16, 6:19	A temple of God. His Spirit (His life) dwells in me.
I Cor. 6:17	Joined to the Lord and am one spirit with Him.
I Cor. 12:27	A member of Christ's body Eph. 5:30.
II Cor. 5:17	A new creature. I am holy, perfect and righteous in Christ. Eph. 4:24
II Cor. 5:18-19	Reconciled to God.
Gal. 3:26-28	A son of God and one in Christ.

Gal. 4:6-7	An heir of God since I am a child of God.
Eph. 1:1	A saint I Cor. 1:2, Phil.1: 1, Col. 1:2.
Eph. 2:10	God's workmanship created in Christ.
Phil. 3:20	A citizen of heaven and seated in heaven right now Eph. 2:6.
Col. 3:3	Hidden with Christ in God.
Col. 3:12	Chosen of God, holy, and dearly loved. Eph. 1:3-4
I Thess. 5:5	A son of light and not of darkness.
Phil. 4:13	Strong in Him. Eph. 6:10
2 Peter 1:3	Have been given all things that pertain to LIFE and Godliness
2 Thess. 3:3	Safe, protected.

Here are more ways that we, as new creations in Christ, are equipped with God's Love for us. We should begin to FOCUS on these truths as well as on the Truths already presented in these chapters.

God LOVES me VOLUNTARILY. *It is not based on anything I do or do not do.* It is UNCONDITIONAL, rich in Mercy and full of Grace. He unconditionally accepts me. Rom. 5:8, Eph.1:3-4, 2:4-5, 1 Jn. 4:9-11.

God LOVES me SACRIFICIALLY. I John 4:9-10 One can sacrifice without loving. I Corinthins13:3 But one cannot love without sacrificing. Christ's Love is sacrificial. John 15:13 God's Sacrificial Love SERVES. Philippians 2: 5-8 God's Sacrificial Love is UNDESERVED. I John 4:10a; Romans 5:8

God's LOVE HEALS me. He is Jehovah Rophi. Exodus 15:26

God's LOVE PROVIDES for me. He is Jehovah-Jireh. Genesis 22:11-14; 22:23

God's LOVE is the love of a Father who PROTECTS me. Psalm 91

God LOVES me the *same* as He loves Christ. John 17:23; 15:9.

God's LOVE for me is ETERNAL and INFINITE. It is so staggering that it surpasses knowledge Ephesians 3:19 with power that is far beyond what we can ask or think Ephesians 3:20. The depth of His care for us is unfathomable. Psalm 139

God's LOVE is my PEACE. Eph. 12:14, Rom. 5:1

God's LOVE is my STRENGTH. Eph. 6:10, Phil. 4:13, Col. 1:11

That is LOVE in The Present Tense

CHAPTER 7

OH - Do You Need a Helper?

Some of us would say we DO.

But those of us who are strong-willed, self-sufficient and take pride in what we do, can reject the very thought of needing "a helper". But those of us who DO need a HELPER as we persevere in *focusing on renewing our minds to truth* during difficult times in this world, might find the following...... HELPFUL.

Jesus speaks of the role of the HOLY SPIRIT that would come to dwell WITHIN a Believer's new spirit *in this, the New Covenant age after His resurrection*, saying the HOLY SPIRIT would be our HELPER. When we are born again, we are joined with Christ who IS the Holy Spirit – and He IS our Helper.

Jesus said...

But I tell you the truth, it is to your advantage that I go away; for if I do not go away, the HELPER will not come to you; but if I go, I will send Him to you. John 16:7 I will ask the Father, and He will **give you another HELPER, that He may be with you** *forever; that is* the SPIRIT of TRUTH, whom the world cannot receive, because it does not see

Him or know Him, *but* you know Him because *He abides with you and will be IN YOU*. John 14:16-17

Jesus said, "the **HELPER, the HOLY SPIRIT**, whom the Father will send in My name, He will teach you all things, and bring to your remembrance all that I said to you. John 14:26 When the HELPER comes, whom I will send to you from the Father, *that is* the SPIRIT OF TRUTH who proceeds from the Father, He will testify about Me." John 15:26

Since the HELPER, who IS the HOLY SPIRIT - the SPIRIT of TRUTH - God's eternal LIFE - lives in Believers, they are "in the spirit", if indeed the SPIRIT of God DWELLS IN them. But if anyone does not have the SPIRIT of CHRIST, he does not belong to Him. Rom. 8:9 He who has the Son HAS the LIFE; he who does not have the Son of God does not have the LIFE. 1 John 5:12   So CHRIST, the HOLY SPIRIT, is the SPIRIT of TRUTH, and is the new LIFE in us, Col. 3:4

And thus, **our HELPER *IS* Christ's SPIRIT of LOVE, LIFE and PEACE –** His Power and Provision and Protection *IN US!*

Also if the SPIRIT of HIM who raised Jesus from the dead DWELLS IN YOU, He who raised Christ Jesus from the dead *will also* give LIFE **to your mortal bodies** through HIS SPIRIT who DWELLS IN you. Rom. 8:11 As we live our daily lives by our old strategies, we won't feel that His life is in us. But it is TRUE.

Referring to after His resurrection, Jesus said, "In that day, you will know I am in My Father, and YOU IN ME, and I IN YOU." He spoke of that mystery, *Christ in you*, the hope of glory. John 14:20, Col. 1:27 So the one who is joined with the Lord is one SPIRIT *WITH HIM*. IF you are a believer, having received Christ... your body is a TEMPLE of God and the SPIRIT of God DWELLS IN YOU whom you have from God, and that *you are not your own*. 1 Cor. 6:17,19

The SPIRIT of LIFE and TRUTH is our HELPER and **resides in our new spirit**. It is BY the Helper that believers **are *equipped*** and ***empowered*** to choose to walk in Him – walk by the Spirit. We are made ***adequate*** to change our minds to walk in Truth. *The Helper was NOT placed in us to help us walk after our own HUMAN WAYS and UNDERSTANDING…not according the fleshly ways that might seem right to our human mind and reason.*

The HELPER equips us to receive God's LOVE so we can relax from our struggling and trying hard to find what we long for. And He is our power to pursue BEING TRANSFORMED in OUR human MIND/ SOUL to His image – HIS MIND-SET - that dwells in our SPIRIT, and to LIVE IT OUT. As a result, we will KNOW Him more fully and experience the things we hope for – joy, peace, security, worth, and a conscience free of guilt. This is the reason we need the Helper

The Definition of Helper

What does the word, "Helper" mean in the New Testament, specifically in reference to the Holy Spirit and our being joined with the Spirit? 1 Cor. 6:17; John 14:16-17, 20; John 3:6 The Greek word for Helper, *boēthos*, means, "strength" and "rescue". The Greek word, *paráklētos*, is "helper" and/or "advocate". *Boēthos* is a noun made up of two words which mean "cry out" or "intense exclamation" and "run". The verb of this word *boētheō* means "come to the rescue" or "supply urgently needed help. In the New Testament where *boēthos* appear, all the verses refer to a strong, rescuing – a divine – help.

Because Jesus paid for the sin that separated us from God and we have been made new creatures in Him, joined with His Life (the Helper) IN us, we CAN live and choose Life...when we make an active choice of our will.

HE resides in our Spirit as a helper who establishes us, strengthens us, equips us, and makes us **adequate to be a doer of God's word, not just a hearer.** He is our strength to walk by faith.

But I say, walk **by the Spirit**, and you will not carry out the desire of the flesh. Gal. 5:16

What incredible reasons to be joined as one - with Christ - Himself.

That is LOVE in The Present Tense

CHAPTER 8

More Reasons We Are Joined with Christ

God doesn't dwell in us –

isn't joined with us in spirit making us new creations - *just for our sake.* Christ isn't our New Life *only* so we will know we are forgiven, will live for eternity with Him, experience peace, freedom from a guilty conscience, and know who we are in Him so we can accept ourselves. That is AWESOME.

> But our knowing our **identity as new creations**,
> joined as one with Him is *just the beginning*!

Equipped and Adequate

The **purpose** of our being JOINED WITH God's LIFE is that He would grant us, according to the riches of His glory, to be *STRENGTHENED with power* through His Spirit in *the inner* man. Eph. 3:16 Believers are joined to Him who was raised from the dead**, in order that** we might ***bear fruit*** for God. Rom. 7:4 Therefore, we are *TO GUARD*, through the Holy Spirit who dwells in us, *THE TREASURE* which has been entrusted to us. 2 Tim. 1:14

The **purpose** is so that the man of God may be ADEQUATE, EQUIPPED for every *GOOD WORK*. 2 Tim. 3:17 God gave us His LIFE and unique abilities/gifts for the equipping of the saints for *the* WORK OF SERVICE, to the *building up of the body* of Christ. Eph. 4:12

By Christ's sacrifice for us and His Spirit in us, we **have been made adequate and are equipped** for **His purpose** as we live in this world. Not that we are adequate in ourselves to consider anything as coming from ourselves, but our ADEQUACY is of God who also made us ADEQUATE *as* SERVANTS of a NEW COVENANT, not of the letter (religious Law) but of the Spirit; for the letter kills, but the Spirit gives life. 2 Cor. 3:4-6

Jesus told His disciples, "Apart from Me, you can do nothing" John 15:5 This means we can do *nothing* regarding Life and Godliness without being empowered by His Spirit in us. BY His Spirit, we are to (choose to) STAND FIRM in the FAITH, be STRONG, and let ALL that WE DO be done IN LOVE. 1 Cor. 16:13-14 We are to choose to be STEADFAST, immoveable, always ABOUNDING IN the WORK *of the Lord* for you know your work is not in vain in the Lord. We are to be DOERS of the word, and not only HEARERS. James 1:22-23, I Corinthians 15:58.

> We should know that we *are* EQUIPPED in every good thing to DO HIS WILL, working in us that *which* is PLEASING in *his sight*, through Jesus Christ, to whom *be* the glory forever and ever. Heb. 13:21 Sometimes we hear that endeavoring to *please God* would be "legalism"- or our trying to earn something good from Him or "pay Him back for doing so much for us."

> But those beliefs are NOT truth and are not possible. Those are NOT the reasons we are to please God. Our being PLEASING to Him is because HE ENJOYS it! He is *pleased* when we

fellowship with Him and know Him. Col. 1:10; Heb. 13:16; 1 Thess. 2:4, 4:1 And we are also delighted in that!

Because we are ONE with Christ, literally in UNION with Him in our spirit, we *can* DO ALL THINGS *through Him who* STRENGTHENS *us*. This does NOT mean we are equipped do just "anything" we might aspire to do. It means ALL things that *pertain to LIFE and GODLINESS*. Paul said for him that meant knowing how to get along with humble means, also know how to live in prosperity; in any and every circumstance he learned the secret of being filled and going hungry, both of having abundance and suffering need. Phil. 4:12-14

Relating to that, we are to know and be AWARE that whoever desires to be Godly WILL BE PERSECUTED. No it doesn't sound like fun. But there is a purpose in it. Receiving the *hard times, and often with persecution*, is part of God's prod for us to **GROW in our perseverance of FAITH expressing itself through LOVE.** We have been made adequate to mature and respond with the mind of Christ in the face of others' insults, rejections, and falsely saying all kinds of evil against us because of Him. We are to rejoice and be glad, for our reward in heaven is great. Matt. 11:12, 1 Peter 3:16

For we are His workmanship, **created in Christ Jesus for** GOOD WORKS which God prepared beforehand so that we would WALK IN them. Eph. 2:10 These are the works for which we are equipped. These are WORKS that result from our OBEDIENCE of FAITH. Rom. 1:5, Rom. 16:26 And they are NOT from our trying to do external works of religious law. No, but the **WORKS** are **by a LAW of FAITH.** Rom. 3:27

It is **by the Helper** that we have been equipped to *grow by exercising our faith* to **express itself by LOVE.** Gal. 5:6 This is our *WORK* of FAITH and *LABOR* of LOVE and steadfastness of hope in our Lord Jesus Christ 1 Thess. 1:3 Our work of FAITH is when we LOVE others, and that IS when we LOVE God and KNOW God. 1 John 4:8

That is LOVE in the Present tense.

CHAPTER 9

It is for Freedom

Recent circumstances

have brought forth some deep and valid concerns about the possibilities of our nation losing many of its freedoms. Our country was founded and established for FREEDOM – for LIBERTY. And we must pray and do what can be done to preserve it.

But there is another way we as believers can live AS IF we are held CAPTIVE. And all of us have been there. It is to be in the "prison" of our own human mind and consciousness. When we are overcome with fear/anxiety, it is AS IF we are held CAPTIVE by fear. If we are obsessed with relationships, accomplishments, finances, etc., as the source of our needs being met, we can feel and live AS IF we are imprisoned - and not realize why.

Often we fear being empty / lonely, and our life consists of trying to do everything we can to "collect" people or to "buy" relationships. Or we strive to do things "right" or be the "best" to be loved, accepted and feel of value. Or we might change locations a lot in an effort to find peace. We can hold grudges or try to escape our emotional pain and grief in various ways. **And nothing works**.

Yes, believers have been SET FREE from the power of sin and death, 1 Cor. 15:56 and Christ's Life in us **empowers** us to **live in** and **enjoy** our FREEDOM. But often without realizing it, believers can *hold themselves* as if they are CAPTIVE to *old beliefs and ways* of trying to fill ourselves, feel secure, significant and content. OR it might be by our trying to live up to religious law.

It can *seem* we are imprisoned by these ways – by our old thinking and programming about how needs are to be met that developed from the power of sin in us, our human nature before our new birth, and the principles of the present world system. These are our FLESHLY strategies. These old ways are not of faith. ***And they do not come from who we are as new creations.*** When we are OVERCOME by these ways, we can live AS IF we are ENSLAVED by them. 2 Pet. 2:19-20 But the Truth is we have been *SET FREE* from the *POWER* of SIN (religious law) and the FLESHLY patterns of thinking and behaving.

The ***power that sin*** had over us has been ***done away with***, so we would ***no longer be slaves*** to sin. Rom. 6:6 It was so sin would **no longer have power** to enslave us. The **power of sin is** the old religious **Law**. 1 Cor. 15:56 But the law of the Spirit of life in Christ Jesus has set you **free from** the **law of sin and of death**. Rom. 8:2

Even though these FLESHLY strategies have **no power** to enslave us, they become OUR *OWN* LAWS for living. Living by them can kill and destroy - just as religious law! This **captivity is in our mind** and happens by our **being deceived** in our thinking as to what will meet our needs and bring what we long for! Rom. 16:18b

We are not to **deceive ourselves** to think it's okay to live by the standards of this world system, 1 Cor. 3:18 Those who fear are perishing emotionally, because they are deceived.

So what is the answer? Jesus said, "He has sent Me to proclaim

RELEASE to the CAPTIVES, and recovery of SIGHT to the BLIND."
Luke 4:18 It was FOR FREEDOM that Christ SET US FREE. Gal. 5:1

You mean we don't have to be held in mental / emotional CAPTIVITY
by sin and guilt, by fear, by shame, by the effects of others mistreating
us, rejecting us, lying about us, crucifying us? Or by our own ways
of thinking and conducting ourselves the best way we know how?
Jesus said, "The things I have spoken to you, are so that in Me you
may have PEACE. In the world you have tribulation, but take courage;
I have overcome the world." John 16:33

We have been set free, but we need to live and walk in that freedom
by knowing truth.

But HOW???

So HOW do we live in the FREEDOM for which Christ came to SET
US FREE? **He said, "You will *KNOW* the truth, and the TRUTH will
make you FREE."** John 8:32 And this is where the **renewing of our
mind** comes in.

The following words of encouragement are reminders of Truths
that were presented earlier. We first need to receive, and renew
our mind, to truth - the truth of God's unconditional LOVE for us,
and that Christ's sacrifice forgave all of our "mess-ups" – past, present and future. We need to **believe** that He set us FREE from the
POWER sin held over us - FREE from our being ENSLAVED by it.
Rom. 6:6; 1 Cor. 15:56 And we need to believe that He abolished
DEATH, which means He ended our SEPARATION from His LIFE
and FREEDOM. 2 Tim. 1:10

We need to believe that when He arose from the grave He sent His
LIFE to forever be joined with the spirit of those who believe, making us new creations – with an identity and power that is from Him

- not from what we do or have. HIS LIFE is unspeakable JOY, PEACE that exceeds our human comprehension, and it is FREEDOM from a guilty conscience. Heb. 9:14; 10:22 It is knowing we are totally and unconditionally accepted by God.

As new creations, we need to KNOW we are made spiritually **adequate** and **complete** in everything that pertains to LIFE and Godliness. 2 Pet.1:3 He became our strength, our security, our provision, our peace, our joy and power. Heb. 9:14; 10:22

We need to KNOW that Christ came and was crucified so that we could be INWARDLY FREE from the enslaving power of sin - from our old FLESHLY patterns of thinking and the principles of this world system - as we live NOW. He gave Himself for our sins so that He might RESCUE us Phil. 3:12 from this PRESENT evil AGE, according to the will of our God and Father, Gal. 1:4

This means He came that we might *experience* - as the outcome of exercising our faith - the inner *salvation of our SOUL*. Our soul is our human mind, will and emotions. As to this salvation, the prophets who prophesied of the grace that would come to you, made careful searches and inquiries, 1 Pet. 9-10

That is a lot of truth to know.. isn't it? And it takes time to focus on it, **renew our mind** to it, walk in it, and grow in it. Especially when our old ways (which can often *look good - even religious*) and the defeating feelings which result from our deceptive thinking, get in the way!

But it is WORTH it, because the truth will open the eyes of our understanding and lead us to experience the FREEDOM that is already ours! We believers do not always *experience* or enjoy what we ALREADY HAVE, do we? But knowing and walking in Truth **destroys *the deceptions* that *seem to hold* us captive** – our old ways of thinking and behaving!

We were given the power of His Spirit to dwell in us so we would be equipped to ACCESS by FAITH this LIFE of Grace and FREEDOM that is ALREADY ours here and now. 2 Cor. 3:6; Rom. 5:2 This LIFE that is eternal – meaning a QUALITY of LIFE that is without end.

Christ revealed the secret – the MYSTERY - of our experiencing or laying hold on this LIFE - the inner Freedom and Liberty that is already ours as believers. Phil. 3:12

> It is by what is called, the perfect law, the Law of LIBERTY. It is also called the Law of the Spirit of Life in Christ. Rom. 8:2 The one who looks intently at the perfect law, the LAW of LIBERTY, and abides by it, **not having become a forgetful hearer but an *effectual doer*,** this man will be blessed in what he does. James. 1:25

This PERFECT LAW of LIBERTY is…. the LAW of LOVE.

As new creations we must learn to trust the power of Christ and His Love in us, and then *by faith* choose to **express His LOVE to others.** This is our effectual *inner* DOING. We do this by focusing on renewing our human mind to Christ's mind-set of LOVE as we walk in our day to day circumstances.

We capture false beliefs by REPLACING THEM with the truth of His sufficiency for us and with HIS MIND-SET – His attitude of humility, being a servant, and preferring others above ourselves. Phil. 2:5-8; Rom 12:10 **That is LOVE.**

When we **walk in LOVE**, we **fulfil the Law of Christ.** Rom. 13:10 Just as He did. Jesus said, "This is My commandment, that **you love one another**, just **as I** have **loved you.**" John 15:12 We are told that perfect (mature) love casts out fear. 1 John 4:18 When we renew our minds to receive His LOVE and then express it toward others, fear is cast aside.

> When we persevere in this, we EXPERIENCE more fully who we ALREADY are in Christ and the FREEDOM, joy, peace and sufficiency we ALREADY have in Him. He overcame for us and equipped us inwardly to overcome – to **walk in this freedom by loving others** in the midst of our fears and the hurtful situations we encounter.

> We *overcome* fear and hopelessness by our faith expressing itself through LOVE - a way that is exactly OPPOSITE of the world's principles that can hold us captive. But it is the only thing that counts... It is when we walk according to the Spirit. Gal. 5:6,16

When we express our faith by LOVE, we overcome evil with good. Rom 12:21 And we delight more completely in our FREEDOM. It can involve hard choices when we fear rejection, are falsely accused, or mistreated and our emotions don't line up immediately. But we have to remember emotions don't represent truth.

And as we persevere and press on in faith expressing itself by LOVE, our feelings will change and we will **lay hold** more thoroughly **on the freedom** and **fullness** that is **already** ours - and in the midst of the trials! Phil. 3:12,14 By this, our own hindrances to partaking of what is ours in Him, are removed. We leave behind those old ways of thinking that led to old behaviors plus any emptiness and anxiety that seemed to enslave us.

Jesus' new and astounding message as He spoke of **the New Covenant that was to come**, was to LOVE your enemies, do good to those who hate you, bless those who curse you, pray for those who mistreat you. Luke 6:27 This can only be done as we remind ourselves of, and rely on, Christ's power and provision that indwells us. We press on with **the attitude of Christ** – and not just by outer behaviors. It is being kind, patient, and forgiving with that *mind of Christ - humility, having the attitude of a servant, and preferring others above ourselves.*

More will be explained in later chapters about letting the mind of Christ in us also be our human mind-set.

This is an ongoing process of learning and growing. But it is when we walk in FREEDOM.

When we walk in this way, it is when **Christ is revealed** in us. It is when we **are being made perfect** (complete) in our human mind/ **soul** as we **have been made perfect** in our **spirit.** It is when we are being transformed – and conformed to His image. It is when we know His Peace. It is our high calling in Christ.

The people in New Testament times thought of being held captive and not being free as being bound by EXTERNAL circumstances. But Jesus spoke here (as He did many times) of an INNER freedom that He came to give us, but He used words / metaphors to which the people could relate that referred to the physical world, *to tell of what was to come under the spiritual / invisible New Covenant.*

It is for FREEDOM that He set us FREE! Gal. 5:1

I am reminded of the following:

Stone Walls do not a Prison make,
Nor Iron bars a Cage;
Minds innocent and quiet take
That for an Hermitage.
If I have FREEDOM in my LOVE,

LOVE IN THE PRESENT TENSE

And in MY SOUL am FREE,
Angels alone that soar above,
Enjoy such LIBERTY.

From: "To Althea, from Prison" in 1642 by Richard Lovelace

That is LOVE in the Present tense.

CHAPTER 10

Set Free to BE...
Owned as Slaves.   Whaaat?!

As believers, we may know who we are in Christ

and that we are totally forgiven forever, made accepted in Him and united as one with Him in our spirit. We may know we have been SET FREE from the POWER of SIN and from the power the world system had over us and that we now have power over the powers of the enemy.

We may also know that the Law of the Spirit of Life in Christ Jesus has set us FREE from the law of sin and death, the POWER that ENSLAVED us, Rom. 8:2, and it was for our *inner freedom* that Christ set us FREE.

But do we know this.... *because* we have been set free, we must **stand firm** and **not be subject again to a yoke of slavery** / bondage? Gal. 5:1 **Whaat?!**

Yes, we believers are told that since we were bought with a price by Christ, we are to not become SLAVES of people. This is referring to the INNER SLAVERY of living after our fleshly ways and the world system. 1 Cor.15:56; Rom 8:2; Gal 5:1; 1 Cor. 7:23

We have been set FREE. But have we realized the significance of the following statements? "We are not our own, we have been bought with a price." "We belong to Christ." "We are His own possession." "We are His children." "We are slaves of righteousness." Have you really thought about that? He OWNS us. Wow. 1Cor. 3:23; 1 Cor. 6:18-20; Titus 2:14; 1Peter 2:9; Acts 17:28; Rom. 6:17,19

Hmmmmm. What does THAT sound like? SLAVERY?

BUT SLAVES aren't always OBEDIENT to their owners.....ARE they?

Did you know that your body is a temple of the Holy Spirit who is in you, whom you have from God, and that you are NOT YOUR OWN because you have been BOUGHT with A PRICE and are SLAVES to Righteousness? 1 Cor. 6:18-20 And **because of this**, we are to glorify God in our BODY. We are told to *flee immorality BECAUSE* we ARE FREE from sin's power and have been made SLAVES to Christ. But it's not only physical immorality that we should flee.

We are even told to let no unwholesome WORD proceed from our mouth, but only such A WORD as is good for EDIFICATION according to the need of the moment, SO THAT it will GIVE GRACE to those who hear. In other words, we are to BE who we already ARE in Christ. We are to be OBEDIENT in the faith, and not be conformed to our former ways. 1 Cor. 6:18; 1 Cor.6:20; Eph. 4:29; Rom. 6:17; Acts 6:7

We believers are FREE. Yet we are Christ's SLAVES. BUT. Now this.

Do we know that when we **offer** OURSELVES to someone as OBEDIENT SLAVES, we are SLAVES of the one whom we OBEY, whether we are slaves to sin, which *leads to death* - or to the **obedience** which *results in righteousness* (Christ's righteousness being outworked - revealed in and through us as we are being conformed to His image)? Rom. 6:16 (The word *death* in this scripture means the *believer's* **separation** from *enjoying in this present world what is ALREADY theirs in Christ* - His peace, joy and a conscience free from guilt),

We *offer* (present) **ourselves** as SLAVES to RIGHTEOUSNESS when we *choose to* LOVE - serve and give ourselves up for others as Christ gave Himself up for the church. **This is when others see Christ in us and desire to know Him as we do**. It is PROOF of our faith to others. Phil. 2:15

In reference to this, the Apostle Paul said, "I am speaking in human terms because of the weakness of your FLESH. For just as you **presented** the parts of your body as slaves to impurity and to lawlessness, resulting in *further* lawlessness, so **now present** your body's parts as *slaves to righteousness*, resulting in sanctification." Rom. 6: 18-22

It is important to know that since we *have been made slaves* to Christ, that we are to *willingly* BE WHO WE ARE and **present ourselves as slaves to righteousness** *which results in our* **experiencing** *the sanctification that we ALREADY have!*

> This means that even though we are slaves to righteousness, we have to **make choices** to walk by faith expressing itself through Love for others. Even when we know our identity in Christ, **our walking according to the Spirit does not come automatically.** It is by choices we are equipped to make.

We are to be obedient in both our MIND and in fleeing immorality in our BODY. Often the definition of a "bond-slave" or "bond-servant" in scripture is one who has **been set free** to **willingly** *place Himself* **back under servitude**. When we do not present ourselves in this way as slaves to righteousness we BLOCK ourselves from experiencing in this life all that is ours in Christ!

In order to do this, we have to be DILIGENT. 2 Peter 3:14, 2 Tim.

2:15 Believers who have received the Spirit of Christ are exhorted to be STEDFAST Heb. 3:6 to our profession of faith. We are told this because we are partakers of Christ IF we are *DILIGENT* to keep our **full assurance of hope** until the end.

This is our **choosing** to ABIDE *(to continue)* in FAITH expressing itself by LOVE. When we do this our fleshly hindrances to partaking more fully of Christ's Life in us are put aside and we - LAY HOLD on - EXPERIENCE more completely in this present age the promises that are ALREADY ours in Christ. Heb. 6:11-12 NIV

We are to HOLD FIRMLY the confession of our hope without wavering, for He who promised is faithful. In doing this, we are to consider how to *stimulate each other* to *LOVE* and *GOOD DEEDS*. The "good deeds" spoken of here are not outer works of trying to obey religious law but are the fruit of **exercising faith to LOVE others** from our heart. Heb. 3:14; 10:23-24 KJV

We aren't told to ***hold fast and stand firm*** *in* **faith** only in our hope of what God can do, and will do, for us. It is our choosing by His power in us to STAND FIRM in our OBEDIENCE of FAITH that is expressed by our LOVE for others in the face of false accusations, temptations, trials and adversity.

Having been freed from sin and ENSLAVED to GOD, it is for OUR BENEFIT that we **stand firm** and not waiver in living out our FAITH, especially in the face of suffering. And it is NOT because we will EARN anything from God by doing so. It is because as we persevere, we are *walking in the power of His resurrection,* are maturing in our *expression of Holiness,* in our *knowing God* and in our *laying hold on* - enjoying now in this present world - the *Eternal Life* we ALREADY have in Him. Rom. 1:5; 6:21-23; 16:26. This is our calling as believers.

> Now that you have been set free from sin and have become slaves of God, the benefit you reap *leads to* holiness, and the result is our enjoying eternal life - now. Rom. 6:22

This can happen only BECAUSE we have ALREADY been unconditionally accepted and empowered by God's Life within us. This kind of obedience is a **choice of the mind / heart** - and it isn't done to find acceptance from humans nor to achieve anything for ourselves. **Wow**.

SO **IF** we who are believers, *having been bought as slaves for righteousness*, choose to continuously walk after old fleshly ways and beliefs (that can look good OR bad) instead of according to the Spirit, we **offer ourselves** as SLAVES to that way – and reap the consequences of it! AND that IS possible.

When we do that, we have *not* stood firm and held fast to our faith, and we will experience the consequences as we live in this present world. We SEPARATE ourselves from partaking or experiencing what we already have in Christ! No. God doesn't condemn us if we do not stand firm in faith. **We will be *condemned by our own conscience*!** And we will live with anxiety and fear. Rom. 6:16; Eph. 6:5-7; 1 Tim. 1:5, Heb.10:22-23

SO, believers are told to **not OFFER** any part of yourself to sin as an instrument of wickedness, but rather **offer yourselves to God** as those who **have been brought** from **death to life**; and **OFFER** every part of yourself to him as an instrument of righteousness. Rom. 6:13 NIV If we continuously offer ourselves to sin, we have received the grace of God IN VAIN!

We urge you NOT to RECEIVE God's grace IN VAIN. For He says, 'In the time of my favor I heard you, and in the day of salvation I helped you.' I tell you, NOW is the time of God's favor, **NOW** is the day of SALVATION. 2 Cor. 1-2 NIV   We must know that Christ came and was crucified, risen, and indwells us so that we could be delivered (SAVED) from the consequences of living in this PRESENT EVIL WORLD. Gal. 1:4

If we do NOT STAND FIRM and PRESS ON in faith, the blessings of the *kingdom within* us are not to our BENEFIT here and now, and we have received His grace IN VAIN. "Not that I have already grasped *it all* or have already become perfect (mature in soul and body), but I **press on** if I may also TAKE HOLD of that for which I WAS even TAKEN HOLD OF by Christ Jesus." Phil. 3:12 This is when we PRESS ON to maturity in Christ. Heb. 6:1

The GOAL of our instruction (concerning this obedience of faith from the heart) is to **LOVE from a pure heart and a good conscience and a sincere faith.** And it is so **our own conscience won't condemn us** and we **won't live in fear**. 1 Tim. 1:5   So let us remember to draw near with a sincere heart in full assurance of faith, having our hearts sprinkled clean from an evil conscience and our bodies washed with pure water. Let us HOLD FAST the confession of our hope without wavering, for He who promised is faithful. Heb. 10:22-23

We walk in and experience the freedom that is already ours when we **stand firm and press on in the likeness – the mind-set – of Christ. That is when we walk in LOVE.**

But just WHAT does that mean? When Christ came, He **revealed what had been hidden** in the Old Covenant - about LOVE. **He revealed a secret.**

That is LOVE in the Present tense.

VIP: Knowing the above, we must understand that our American view of slavery is different than in Biblical times.   Certain translations of scripture use the word "SERVANT" rather than "SLAVE" in some scriptures. But the Hebrew perspective was behind Jesus' "slave-language" because He was speaking to those under the Old Covenant and wanted them to understand what to "follow Him" meant.   He knew they would understand what He meant by using the word "slave" when he used it to refer to an INNER attitude, because they understood what "slave" meant outwardly.

CHAPTER 11

Christ Revealed a Secret

Are you ready for it?

There was a KEY – to a MYSTERY. **It was an explanation as to HOW God's LIFE could be experienced and lived out in people's lives,** but it **had been HIDDEN in God** and **in Old Testament Law**. This secret was not revealed during the time of the Old Testament (old Mosaic covenant). Matt. 13:35; Eph. 3:9b When Jesus arrived, He not only fulfilled God's Old Testament Law on our behalf, (Matt. 5:17) He REVEALED in parables that the secret to God's law being lived out through us *is* **to love one's neighbor as one's self.**

Christ's sacrificial death fulfilled the Old Covenant law once and for all time on our behalf. AND – believers need to know this – **the law is also *fulfilled in those who love*** *others* – which is loving others with God's love. Rom. 13:8,10; Gal. 5:14; James 2:8 That is BIG. As was presented earlier chapters, it was only after His resurrection - after He ascended into Heaven - that God sent His Spirit to *dwell in* believers making them *adequate* to walk after the Spirit and live out God's *agapao* love....and thus for the law to be fulfilled by them!

Since Christ met the requirements of the law on our behalf, God DOES NOT punish or condemn us if we do not walk after the spirit and mature in love. But scripture tells us it *is for our benefit* that we are called and exhorted to walk in LOVE – **to obey** in this way "for you were called for the very purpose that *you might inherit a bless-ing*." I Peter 3: 9b I will say that again... It is for OUR BENEFIT. When we don't walk in love WE *block* our fullest *experience* here and now of what is already ours in Christ!

In the Old Testament, religious metaphors were outward, *external* set-tings, objects and behaviors. They were visible symbols or allegories that spoke of *internal,* invisible, spiritual truths that would be revealed in the New Testament (new covenant) age that was to come. Since God is a Spirit, the way into the holiest place of knowing Him spiritu-ally had not yet been disclosed or brought to light. It hadn't occurred to people that there was actually a way to know God.

The people believed the old law was in reference to external behav-iors, so they had tried to keep / obey the law by performance to avoid God's wrath. But in disclosing that the Old Testament law wasn't kept by one's outer actions, Jesus **revealed the secret** of how it *is* to be lived out by giving a "new commandment".

A New Commandment

He said, "A **new commandment** I give to you, that you love one another, even as I have loved you, that you also love one another." John 13:34; John 15:12 YET he also said, " Beloved, I am **not** writing **a new commandment** to you, but an **old commandment** which you have had from the begin-ning; the **old commandment** is the word which you have heard. On the other hand, I **am** writing **a new commandment** to you, which is true in Him and in you, because the darkness is passing away and the true Light is already shining." I John 2:7-8 **Does it sound confusing?**

Well when He said it *is not* new, he meant that *both* His new commandment and the old commandments *are the same.* When He said His commandment *is* new, He meant it in the sense that the people were seeing for the first time that **love** is how the whole law is carried out or fulfilled. This was NEW information, *a new revelation*, to the people. His commandment was NEW because *instead of referring to outer visible behaviors, it revealed an inner obedience* - the *purifying of one's heart* (SOUL) to **love** others I Peter 1:22 *which is the key* to keeping all of the Commandments. And it is **the key** to pressing on in the **obedience of faith.**

They learned that **love** does no wrong to a neighbor; therefore **love** is the way all of *the* old **law is fulfilled**! Rom 13:10 In other words, in the course of our LOVING God *BY* our loving others, ALL of the commands ARE kept in the process - as a "side-effect", so to speak!

The people had never heard that! It was NEW because it spoke of the power of the internal and invisible *realm of the Spirit* - things above / beyond the visible world. The old commandments were words (letters) written on physical, visible stone tablets, but *under the new covenant, we learn that the commandments are of the Spirit and written on the heart.* 2 Cor. 3:3 This was NEW. Christ didn't come to abolish the law but to fulfill the law for those who believe. Matt. 5:17 By His sacrifice and by revealing the secret of keeping the old commandments, the Mosaic covenant was made *obsolete for believers*. Heb. 8:13 Everything under the old covenant, and everything prophesied before Christ, pointed to the revealing of these secrets and other hidden truths, and to our spiritually possessing God's promises.

The old is gone and the new has come.

Christ **made us adequate** *as **servants*** of a *new covenant, (which is)* not of the letter (the old Mosaic covenant's written commandments) but of the Spirit; for the **letter kills,** but the **Spirit gives life.** 2 Cor. 3:6

Trusting God and intentionally ***putting on our new self*** means to be **conformed** in our heart (soul / mind) to the **likeness of Christ** who already dwells in our Spirit and to allow this likeness to work out in daily circumstances. This is the RENEWING of our MIND – to His likeness and mind-set.

That is the meaning of Jesus' statement, "You shall love the Lord your God with all of your HEART, and with all of your SOUL, and with all of your MIND. This is the great and foremost commandment. The second is like it *(is the same thing)*, you shall love your neighbor as yourself." Matt. 22:37; Luke 10:24-19 The people had never heard the explanation.

Those two commandments mean the same thing – that when we love others we ARE loving God. A person may say he/she loves Jesus, but it often means they love Him *for what he has done,* and for what He *gives,* which is tremendous, but we *know* we love God when we love others. 1 John 4:7 This is also seen in Matt. 25:40.

After Christ's resurrection and Pentecost, believers began to understand that they had been given *freedom* from the bondage of the law, the power of sin and a guilty conscience. They were seeing that the hidden key of LOVE had been revealed to them. **The MYSTERY had been REVEALED**. And they would learn that LOVE could only be lived by the power of Christ's *life - **His Spirit*** within us. Because of this new revelation of how the law is to be fulfilled, Jesus' commandment to Love others is also called, **the law of the Spirit of life in Christ Jesus** Rom 8:2 and **the perfect law of liberty / freedom**. Jas. 1:25 To love others (meet the requirement of the *law of Christ*) IS to **walk according to the Spirit**. Rom. 8:4

Wow.. now THAT is COLOSSAL. Most believers haven't heard that they are under the Law of the Spirit of Life in Christ, the PERFECT LAW of FREEDOM.

"Now to Him who is able to establish you according to my gospel and the preaching of Jesus Christ, according to the **revelation of THE MYSTERY which has been KEPT SECRET for long ages past, but now is manifested**, and by the Scriptures of the prophets, according to the commandment of the eternal God, has been made known to all the nations, **leading to obedience of faith."** The **obedience of faith** is our intentionally **exercising faith to walk in love**. It is our *inner* discipline of the heart. Rom.16: 25-26

> Our **obedience of faith** is to **WALK IN LOVE** just as Christ also loved us and gave Himself up for us, being an offering and a sacrifice to God. Eph. 5:2 *It is by our sacrifice of loving others that the law is fulfilled in us and we will be known as His disciples as Christians.* John 13:35 *It is when we offer up ourselves as spiritual sacrifices.* I Peter 2:5 If we **love one another**, God's power resides in us, and His **love** is perfected in us – in our human mind/soul. I John 4:12 When we love others with God's *agapao* love, we know we have been born of God, and we **KNOW GOD**. 1 John 4:7

The message that Christ taught from the beginning is that we are to love one another. I John 3:11 By this we are being **conformed to His image and likeness!** *Exercising this obedience of faith PURIFIES our SOUL / heart.* Thus we are to sincerely love one another from the heart. I Peter 1:22 We are to speak and act as those who are to be judged by *the* **law of liberty** *(freedom)*. James 2:12

Did you notice that last statement? It stated that **believers** are **judged** by the LAW of LIBERTY which is the "new commandment" - **the law of love!** I heard someone say, "Since Christ fulfilled the law on our behalf, we don't have to." But the word says *our loving another is fulfilling the law*. Rom. 13:8,10

LOVE is a fruit of the vine, Christ's Spirit in us. And separate from the Spirit, *we can do nothing* pertaining to LIFE and Godliness - such as loving others. It is only by *His Power in us*, that we can fulfill His commandment to LOVE. It happens *according to the power that works in us*. Eph. 3:20 John 15:4-5 says that since He is the vine and we are the branches, that believers are to ABIDE – to continue – in Him and they will bear much fruit of the spirit.

It is by our abiding - continuing in - faith being expressed by LOVE that we MATURE.

We often categorize *agapao* LOVE as only *one aspect* of the Christian life. But ALL of the METAPHORS and phrases that are used such as *pressing on, running the race, taking Christ's yoke*, etc. refer to our persevering in being *transformed and conformed in our human mind to His image and likeness,* to His mind-set that dwells in our spirit (Rom. 12:2; Phil. 3:10). It is being conformed to the attributes of LOVE. ***This is the ultimate intention of the Christian life**.* It is when we are **being** His witnesses. It is when we are Christ's disciples.

Our growing in love toward others is choosing for *our* FAITH (the faith that expresses itself through **love**) be lived out through us. Gal. 5:6 This **obedience of faith** is empowered by His indwelling life (love) in us. It is not human faith. It is by "...Him who is able to do far more abundantly beyond all that we ask or think, according to the power that works within us." Eph. 3:20 Not that we are adequate to consider anything as coming from ourselves, but our adequacy is of God. II Cor. 3:5

Love defers and lays down itself for others, which make us triumphant. It is opposite of the way the world system triumphs.

Sooo...**TO LOVE** means to press on in exercising Faith. It means to grow up and mature in Christ. It means to put on Christ. It means to pursue righteousness. To pursue Life and Godliness. To abide (continue in). *It all means the same thing – the outworking and expression of what we ALREADY have.* And we have been EQUIPPED to do this by **Christ's Life and Mind-set** in us.

Now...Just what IS the Mind of Christ?

That is LOVE in the Present Tense

CHAPTER 12

Practice LOVE –
by Christ's Mind-set

Living from Christ's mind-set of LOVE

is the only way by which His Life is REVEALED in and through us
Phil. 2:5-8; 2 Peter. 1:10

In order to PRACTICE – which means to CONTINUE IN our living out
- the LOVE and LIKENESS of Christ, Phil. 4:9; 2 Peter 1:10, one must
remember that it happens by intentionally re-training our thinking to
HIS **attitude.** This walk doesn't take place by just **mental re-program-ming** nor by **behavior modification.**   By the power of Christ's Spirit in
us, it is a *discipline to press on* in *focusing* on truth, on *things above,
as we live in daily life and relationships.* This discipline is trusting
and relying on Christ's person, power and promises and allowing His
ATTITUDE or His LIKENESS - to be lived out.

This is our **obedience** and **"putting on" our new self.** Eph. 4:24; Col
3:10 When we are born of the Spirit, our new self, or new nature, is
created in the LIKENESS of God in righteousness and holiness of the
truth. Eph. 4: 23-24   We emphasize again the exhortation to *"put on
the new self"* means to be conformed in our human mind (our soul

/ heart) to that *LIKENESS of God who ALREADY dwells in our Spirit.* His likeness or mind-set is LOVE. This is when Christ is formed in us Gal. 4:19 and **His likeness** is **REVEALED** through us.

What *IS* the LIKENESS of GOD?

Jesus told His disciples that when they *saw Him,* they were *seeing the Father* and if they came to *know Him,* they would *know the Father* God! John 14:7   He said He and the Father God *are one* (spirit). John 10:30   Jesus is the radiance of His Father's glory and the exact representation of His nature. Heb.1:3a *They saw, and we can see, the* **likeness of God** the Father **when we see Christ** in scripture.

God IS LOVE, but how else do we describe the likeness – the heart / mind / power of God?   *It is revealed in the mind-set of Christ.*   And born again believers are told to **let this same mind also be in us**. Phil. 2: 5-8 This **attitude** of Christ *is just the opposite* of the natural way or world's way of thinking.   It is seen in His choosing to **empty Himself** (become of no reputation, KJV), take the form of a **bond-servant**, and **humble Himself** by becoming obedient to the point of death.   Phil. 2:5-8 This is *the likeness of God.*   And it is **Godliness.** Can you imagine our emptying ourselves of who we are for others - as Jesus did?

The Attitude / Mind of Christ = His Likeness:

He emptied Himself. Being fully God *and* fully man, Christ *had no sin or fleshly ways* to void Himself of. He knew Who He was, but *didn't use His IDENTITY to His own advantage*. But He emptied Himself as He lay aside His importance. He GAVE HIMSELF UP for us. Gal. 2:20, Eph. 5:2, 25 Christ chose to become as one without distinction or honor among people. He was willing to be disregarded. He didn't try to protect or promote His reputation or justify Himself. He did not protest because he was mistreated. He didn't try to "save face" or His physical life even though he could. He did not do this on His own initiative, but by the power of the Father working in Him. John 5:30; 8:28; 8:42

He took the attitude of a bond-servant. In Roman times, the term *bond-servant* could refer to someone who *voluntarily served* others. A bond-servant is a person devoted to another to the disregard of one's own interests and who voluntarily **submits to and serves** others, regarding others as more important than him/herself. Mark 10:45; Luke 22:27 The word *bond-servant* comes from the Greek word *doulos*. Being a bond-servant does not mean being a "people-pleaser" who tries to find acceptance, peace and worth by "pleasing" others. Eph. 6:6

He humbled Himself. He didn't try to elevate Himself or find approval and significance by His performance or from people. When he was insulted, He didn't try to "win", or demand His rights to be respected as God. He didn't take up offenses, retaliate or return insults. He blessed those who cursed Him. Christ didn't brag. He chose to be meek, gentle and patient. Matt. 11:

"Even the Son of Man **did not come to be served**, but **to serve**, and to give His life as a ransom for many." Mark 10:45 Jesus sitting down, called the twelve and said to them, "If anyone wants to be first, he shall be last **of all** and **servant of all**." Mark 9:35

Think about it… This Attitude of Christ *is* **THE LIKENESS OF GOD -** a picture of *God Himself* - a description of the Power of God - the *power* that created all that was created and works all things after the counsel of His will! This mind-set describes the *power* of light itself. John 1: 9-10 Those words in Phil. 2: 5-8 describe His *power* on the cross over all the powers of the enemy! Jesus demonstrated that *His power of overcoming is* found in *"losing" - in humility and submission* - that seeming paradox.

The above **mind of Christ** – His attitude – is the essence of **LOVE,** **which is the likeness of God and the power in all of God's attri-** **butes.** God's nature is described in various ways. Good. Faithful. Just. A Shield. Sovereign. Holy. Righteous. Unchanging. All knowing. All Powerful. Present everywhere. Scripture says that all things were made subject to Him. God / Christ is HEAD over all things for His body of believers. Eph. 1:22, I Cor. 11:3 And **GOD** is **LOVE.** (I John 4:8) *And walking in His likeness IS TO LOVE.*

Three Words

Of the many words used to describe *the likeness of God / Christ*, let's look at three words which have very similar Greek meanings. The words are *HEAD, SUBMIT* and *LOVE.* They describe God's very nature – **His likeness**.

> 1. **HEAD** *(Gr: Kephale)* - Col. 1:18; Eph. 4:15 Christ is Head**.** At the time scripture was written, this word for *head* meant *point-man.* A point-man was a soldier who *volunteered to serve*, to LEAD OUT in front of his army - out into an open place - to help them locate where the enemy was. In doing so, he would likely be killed by the enemy. He *died*, sacrificing himself for them. Another word for *head* is the Greek word, *Arche,* which means *boss* or one *having authority over.* Even though *Christ has authority* over all things, **He exercised His authority by choosing to lead out in becoming as a servant and give Himself up** - a *Kephale.* All of this is what LOVE means. That is an ENORMOUS truth.

2. **SUBMIT** (*Gr: Hupotassomai*) - is in the imperative, middle voice - meaning to serve, support, be responsive to, be at the disposition of another. (Another word in the Greek for submit is *Peitharchaeo* – meaning obedience to one in authority.) All of this is to LOVE.   Matt. 20:28; Mark 10:45

3. **LOVE** (*Gr: Agapao*) – is God's Love. It is an attitude resulting in action. It is to voluntarily *serve*, be *responsive to*, to care for in the ways the scripture defines *Love*. " Love is patient, love is kind *and* is not jealous; love does not brag and is not arrogant, does not act unbecomingly; it does not seek its own, is not provoked, does not take into account a wrong suffered, does not rejoice in unrighteousness, but rejoices with the truth; bears all things, believes all things, hopes all things, endures all things." I Cor. 13: 4-7   God IS Love. I John 4:8; 4:16; John 13:34; 15:12

The **LIKENESS** (the mind-set) of Christ is LOVE.

As was stated in Chapter 1, there are normally **three Greek words** for **LOVE** in the New Testament. One of the words is, **Phileo**, meaning, *brotherly love or* friendship. **Storge** has a similar meaning, but refers to having affection as for family members. And the other word is, **Agapao**, which refers to **God's love** and is usually referred to in these writings. (Another Greek word, *Eros*, means *sexual love / attraction*, but this particular word is not mentioned in the New Testament.)

The things you have learned and received and heard and seen in me, **PRACTICE** (continue in) these things, and the God of PEACE will be with you. Phil. 4:9   This means you will ENJOY the PEACE you ALREADY have. Therefore, brethren, be all the more **diligent** to *make certain* about His calling and choosing you; for as long as you PRACTICE these things, you will never stumble. 2 Peter 1:10 Jesus was referring to what humans would be enabled to do under the coming New Covenant when He said, "Take my **yoke** (constraint) upon you **and learn from Me**, for I am **gentle** and **humble** in heart (His **yoke**), and you will find REST for your soul." Matthew 11:29

The Apostle Peter said to the believers, "Since you have in **obedience to the truth** PURIFIED your SOULS for a sincere **LOVE** of the brethren, fervently love one another from the heart, because you **have been** born again not of seed which is perishable but imperishable, that is, through the living and enduring word of God. 1 Peter 1:22 This is when we are being conformed to Christ's image / likeness **in our SOUL.**

Regarding one's spiritual identity and loving others: Our **identity as a new creation** - Christ in us - is **the power** in us to which the Word awakens us. We are to KNOW this - **but that is just the beginning!** The *focus must be on* **choosing** by His power in us to **have the same mind-set in our *human mind*** as the mind of Christ that dwells in our spirit. It is to have our mind set on LOVING others, which is our **obedience of faith.**

> Someone recently said that if believers know their new identity - who they are in Christ - then they ***will automatically know what to do***. If that were true, they would not have these instructions given to them in the written word to renew their minds to the same mind-set as the indwelling Christ, and then be strongly urged to persevere and mature in living out that LOVE toward others.

When we *as believers* try to control our lives, either passively or aggressively, to find what we think will help us and our family be secure and fulfilled, it makes sense to one's *human way of understanding*. But it backfires and leads to conflicts. God's *Agape' LOVE is* **opposite the fleshly or world's way** *of approaching life.*

Jesus said, "You **love one another**, **just as** I have loved you." John 13:34   That means to "Walk in love, **just as** Christ also loved you and **gave Himself up** for us, an *offering and a sacrifice* to God as a fragrant aroma." Eph. 5:2 When we love in this way we "give preference to **one another** in honor." Rom. 12:10 We aren't to put ourselves and desires ahead of them. When we learn to defer to them and serve them instead of ourselves, it might seem a little scary at first. But it is BY THIS, that we will REIGN in life. It is to LIVE out the LIFE of Christ.

These truths remain **a mystery** to the world system!

These truths are the essence of the ***POWER THAT REIGNS through*** *humility, patience, being a servant and not drawing attention to one's self.* It is the VERY OPPOSITE of the way the world's system and the natural human thinks of what it is to have POWER.

Lewis Gregory, President of *Source Ministries International*, conveyed it so well when he said, "In a day when Christians are talking more about their identity in Christ, there is so little about *the outworking of the Christ-life*. Love in the present tense for daily living is a must."

Remember, we can serve without loving, but we cannot LOVE others without serving. It is the intent and attitude of our heart/mind that makes the difference.

Let EVERYTHING you do be done in LOVE 1 Cor. 16:13-14

That is LOVE in The Present Tense

CHAPTER 13

Ready to Go Further with LOVE?

Go further: GROW in Faith and Love

One who has looked intently at the **perfect law**, the **LAW** OF **FREEDOM** – the law of **LOVE** and has **continued** *in it*, not having become a forgetful hearer but an **active doer**, this person will be blessed in what he does. James 1:25

We have written about FREEDOM in earlier chapters, and have conveyed that the LAW of FREEDOM is the LAW of LOVE. So we are to SPEAK, and so ACT, as those who are to be judged by *the* **law** of **freedom,** James 1:25; 2:12 , **the Law of LOVE**. (Now that is another mystery…that we are judged but never condemned!) *So we have been* **set free** *to LOVE and FULFILL that LAW of CHRIST.* James 2:8 When we LOVE is when we KNOW God. 1 John 4:7 AND when we LOVE others, it is our LOVING GOD.

Be on your guard so that you are not carried away by the error of unprincipled men and fall from your own steadfastness. GROW IN the GRACE and KNOWLEDGE of our Lord and Savior Jesus Christ. 2

Peter 3:17-18 We are to go further - GROW and mature – in LOVE – in KNOWING Him.

Many believers haven't even heard about the division of Spirit, Soul and Body… Haven't heard that a believer's goal is to be MATURING in one's human mind - their soul - and being transformed there - to His likeness and completeness that ALREADY dwells in their Spirit…and to live out that attitude so the world may see Christ and believe. It is in this way that God is glorified. All of this is done by a willful **obedience of faith expressing** itself **through love**. Gal. 5:6

Another reminder - in order to GROW and mature in FAITH and LOVE, we first need to realize who we are in Christ and His sufficiency and security for us and renew our mind to that. And then, we *must learn what His indwelling mind-set is in our spirit and begin to think with that same attitude* – which is to LOVE. This is the way we know and experience Him and all He has for us more perfectly.

We are exhorted to be renewed in the spirit of our mind (in our soul), and PUT ON the NEW SELF, which in *the likeness of* God HAS (*already*) BEEN created (in our spirit) in righteousness and holiness of the truth. Eph. 4:24, Col. 3:10   We are to BE transformed in our mind/soul to the likeness of who we already ARE in our Spirit.

 So our "putting on the new self" is our being transformed by the renewing of our mind to Christ's attitude of LOVE.

Knowing one's *identity* in Christ as a NEW CREATION and what we already have in Him is the BEGINNING. **And it is *not to be used for our own advantage*.** It is *our being EQUIPPED* by His Spirit – the Helper - to mature – to DISCIPLINE ourselves in our obedience of faith in the face of difficulties and persecution. It is like a race we run with perseverance and the prize being one's laying hold more fully on Knowing God and the power of His resurrection and the fellowship of His sufferings, being conformed to His death. Phil. 3:10

In doing this we are **not to look to our own interests** but each of us **to the interests of the others.** In all of our relationships with one another, we are to have the **same mindset** as Christ Jesus, which is LOVE. *And this usually happens in the context of adversity and hard times which God uses as a prod for us to exercise faith that expresses itself through LOVE.*

Again, that mind-set of Christ:

> Who, being in very nature God, did not consider equality with God something to be *used to his own advantage*; rather, he made himself nothing by taking the very nature of a servant, being made in human likeness. And being found in appearance as a man, he humbled himself by becoming obedient to death—even death on a cross. Phil. 2:4-8 NIV

We are to let our attitude and goal be the same as the apostle Paul when he said, "I want to *KNOW CHRIST*—that I may know Him and the POWER of His RESURRECTION and the FELLOWSHIP of HIS SUFFERINGS, being CONFORMED to HIS DEATH; in order that I may attain to the resurrection from the dead. NOT that I have already obtained *it* or have already become PERFECT, but I press on so that I may LAY HOLD OF that for which also I *WAS* LAID HOLD of by Christ Jesus.

Brethren, I do not regard myself as having laid hold of *it* yet; but one thing *I do*: forgetting what *lies* behind and reaching forward to what *lies* ahead, I PRESS ON toward THE GOAL for *the prize* of the upward call of God in Christ Jesus. Let us therefore, as many as ARE PERFECT (mature), have THIS ATTITUDE; and if in anything you have a different attitude, God will reveal that also to you. Phil. 3:9-15.

This PRESSING ON even in the face of trials, is spoken of in metaphor as a race we run toward a goal. It is an INNER race of FAITH expressing itself by Love and the fruit of the Spirit. Therefore, since we have so great a cloud of witnesses surrounding us, let us also LAY ASIDE every encumbrance and the sin which so easily entangles us, and let us RUN with ENDURANCE the RACE that is set before us. Heb. 12:1 As we FOCUS on the goal of loving with His mind-set, any sin or hindrances will fall aside or are laid aside - AS A RESULT. So we must not try to *focus on putting them away*.

All of us, then, who are MATURE should take such a view of things. And if on some point you think differently, that too God will make clear to you. Only let us LIVE UP TO what we have ALREADY attained. Phil. 3:10-16   We then LAY HOLD of, in our human experience, what is ALREADY ours in Christ by pressing on in FAITH that expresses itself by LOVE.

As believers, we have been made adequate to do this and to BUILD UP each other in LOVE - maturing in Christ and reaching the same goal... which is until we ALL attain to the unity of the faith, and of the KNOWLEDGE of the SON OF GOD, to a MATURE man, to the measure of the stature which belongs to the FULLNESS of Christ. Remember that our **maturing in LOVE is** to **know God** more completely.

For this reason, we are NO LONGER to BE CHILDREN, tossed here and there by waves and carried about by every wind of doctrine, but to *grow up in all aspects* INTO HIM who is the head, *even* Christ, from whom the whole body, being fitted and held together by what every joint supplies, according to the proper working of each individual part, causes the growth of the body for the building up of itself **in love.** Eph. 4:14-16

It must be said that if we fail to choose to grow up in Him, *He doesn't*

condemn us. He loves and accepts us just the same. But we do not *experience* KNOWING Him more fully.

Scripture refers to various stages of spiritual growth for believers using the terms, *babies, children, young men,* and *fathers.* Those of us who are young in faith are exhorted by scripture to grow so we won't continue to be deceived by the ways of the world. Eph. 4:14-15 We believers who are spiritually immature, "walk after the flesh". This means walking after our false beliefs, or by religious rules, by our own understanding Prov. 3:5 and according to the world system with its ways and desires, which *can* look good and right. But the natural consequences of this path are anxiety, fear, conflict, defeat, self-condemnation, blame of others and separation from enjoying God's peace and joy.

It is God's desire that we be delivered - **saved** - from those consequences of this present evil age Gal. 1:4 and enjoy the freedom He ALREADY has given us. So scripture encourages us to **grow in respect to this salvation,** I Peter 2:2 because the *outcome of our maturing in faith* is *this* **salvation of our soul.** I Peter 1:9 We are told to grow up into him **until Christ be formed in us.** Eph. 4:15; Gal. 4:19 That means our being transformed and conformed in our soul (heart/ mind) to His likeness of LOVE that dwells in our spirit. Because of this we are told to be mature in our thinking I Cor. 14:20 and prepare our **minds** for action! I Peter 1:13

> Spiritual growth is to be highly desired, because without it, believers will continue to walk in defeat in life and relationships. Gal. 4:1 tells us that an *heir of Christ (a believer), as long as he is a child, isn't any different than a slave - because he isn't experiencing the freedom that is already his in Christ!* Our growing to the stage of spiritual maturity is often referred to in scripture as being **perfect** or **complete**.

Those words, "perfect" and "complete" as they are used, mean **mature**. *They do not mean being sinless or without fault or failure. The **goal of our growth is to be** perfected in Love I John 4:17,18 (in our mind / soul) so that we share His likeness / holiness. Eph. 4:24; Heb.12:10 Our growing in LOVE is Godliness!*

Since in scripture spiritual growth is often explained in terms of physical growth, we are to allow babies to be babies and children to be children, and so on.... but we are to encourage them to grow.   Growth takes time.   Maturing and growing spiritually is a process that lasts for the rest of our lives.

So do NOT BE CONFORMED to this WORLD, but BE TRANSFORMED by the renewing of your (human) mind to Christ's attitude of LOVE. **But...again, WHY?**

Here are some reminders as to WHY:

SO THAT you may PROVE (to others) what the WILL of GOD IS...that which is GOOD, ACCEPTABLE and PERFECT. Rom. 12:12   So that they (others) might be JOINED TO HIM who was raised from the dead in order THAT they might BEAR FRUIT FOR GOD. Rom 7:4

SO THAT they who live might NO LONGER LIVE for THEMSELVES, but FOR HIM who died and rose again on their behalf. 2 Cor. 5:15 **SO THAT** the WORLD MAY KNOW that the Father sent Jesus, and the Father LOVED THEM the same as He loves Jesus. John 17: 21-23

SO THAT the LIFE OF JESUS also MAY BE MANIFESTED IN our BODY. For we who live are *constantly being delivered over to death for Jesus' sake* so that the LIFE OF JESUS also MAY BE MANIFESTED IN our MORTAL FLESH. 2 Cor. 4:9-11

We ARE light, and when we GROW UP in Christ, is when we LET our LIGHT SHINE before men in such a way **SO THAT** they may see our GOOD WORKS (Love), and GLORIFY our FATHER who is in heaven. Matt. 5:16 This is when we GROW and are being **perfected in LOVE**.

SO THAT you will PROVE yourselves to be blameless and innocent, children of God above reproach in the midst of a crooked and perverse generation, among whom you APPEAR AS LIGHTS in the world. Phil. 2:15

SO THAT I may LAY HOLD OF that for which also I *WAS* LAID HOLD of by Christ Jesus. Phil. 3:10-15; 2 Peter 1:3

SO THAT I may KNOW GOD. 1 John 4:7-8; John 17:3

You may know what Christ has done for you, who you are in Him, and who He is in you, but that is **the beginning**. The **only way others will know who you are in Christ is by your fruit** - your **growing up** in **LOVE** – bearing the Fruit of the Spirit. John 13:35   When your Faith expresses itself thru Love, your faith is not in vain. The fruit of the Spirit and Love in your life VALIDATES your words to others about Christianity. And by growing in LOVE we enjoy and PARTAKE MORE FULLY of God's Eternal Life that ALREADY indwells us.

Maturing in Faith

The goal of our being equipped

Our MATURING in FAITH is when our *FAITH IS PROVED to others by* our *LOVE* and the fruit of the spirit. This PROOF OF our FAITH, is more precious than gold which is perishable because it results in praise and glory and honor at the revelation of Jesus Christ. When His life in us is revealed through us, then we also will be revealed with Him in His glory. 1 Peter 1:7

That is "the prize" and the reward for those who run the race of faith. It is the assurance of what we hope for. Our hope is not in physical things – but for these things not seen. As we PRESS ON in this obedience of faith being our FOCUS, our FLESHLY HINDRANCES to accessing and experiencing more completely the indwelling grace, joy, peace and unconditional acceptance that is ALREADY ours, are laid aside. This is when we are being **conformed to His** indwelling **image**. It is our FIGHTING the good FIGHT of FAITH; our TAKING HOLD of the ETERNAL LIFE to which we were called 1 Tim. 6:12, and which is ALREADY ours in Christ. And we take hold of it now in this present world.

FAITH *without* WORKS is *useless*, for just as the body without the spirit is dead, so also faith without works is dead. You see that faith was working with his works, and as a result of the works, FAITH was PERFECTED. James 2: 18-26

This standing firm in our FAITH being expressed outwardly by LOVE is **our training in righteousness**. It is when the sanctification we ALREADY have is *being made experiential* in our SOUL. 2 Cor. 3:16 We **have been sanctified entirely** by God's love and grace. But since we are triune beings, our sanctification is to be *manifest from the invisible fact to be appropriated / experienced / revealed* now in time - experienced in and through us - as we walk in the obedience of faith by the power of the spirit. When we think and walk in this way, after a while we find that our emotions have begun to change and we have joy and peace we never had. How awesome is THAT?

> The only thing that matters is our FAITH expressing itself through LOVE. Gal. 5:6 That is our Obedience of Faith. It is our WORK of FAITH and LABOR of LOVE and STEADFASTNESS of HOPE in our Lord Jesus Christ in the presence of our God and Father. Gal. 5:6; 1 Thess. 1:3 So let us CONSIDER how to stimulate one another to LOVE and GOOD DEEDS. Heb. 10:24

The truth now is made manifest, and by the Scriptures of the prophets, according to the commandment of the eternal God, has been made known to all the nations, LEADING to OBEDIENCE of FAITH. Rom. 16:26

Since you have in OBEDIENCE to the truth PURIFIED your SOULS for a sincere LOVE of the brethren, fervently love one another from the heart, 1 Peter 1:22 Whoever KEEPS HIS WORD, in him the LOVE of God has truly been PERFECTED. 1 John 2:5 (Remember one's soul is where one's beliefs, attitudes and emotions exist.)

Biblically, to "be perfect" DOESN'T mean to be without sin. First of all, we can just know that trying to live up to RELIGIOUS LAWS makes NOTHING PERFECT! (Heb. 7:9) The Hebrew word for PERFECT (*tam* or *tamim*) doesn't mean, "without flaw", as the word "perfect" does in English. It usually means COMPLETE or MATURE. The equivalent Greek term in the New Testament (*telos*) means the same thing. Someone, can be maturing or being made complete, yet not be "without flaw."

All Scripture is inspired by God and profitable for teaching, for re-proof, for correction, for **training in righteousness**; so that the man of God may be adequate, equipped for every GOOD WORK. 2 Tim. 3:16-17Top of Form Therefore, my beloved brethren, be STEADFAST, UNMOVABLE, ALWAYS ABOUNDING in the WORK of the Lord, for-asmuch as you know that your LABOR is not in vain in the Lord." 1 Cor. 15:58

Since Jesus Christ is the LIGHT of the world, **when we mature in Faith,** we believers **let our light shine** before others, SO THAT they may see our good deeds and glorify our Father in heaven. Matt. 5:16; Phil. 2:15

That is LOVE in The Present Tense

CHAPTER 14

Humility - Love Expressed

In our culture, humility

is generally seen as undesirable. We live in a day where promoting one's self, improving one's self, being the best, having to be heard and/or right, demanding respect and winning are focal points in life. I just heard someone who won a huge award say, "This has been the joy of my life." These are all efforts to satisfy and build up one's self.

Ego and **pride** reign, but any fulfillment that accolades might bring is fleeting. In some other cultures, individuals take *pride in humility*! Even as believers, we can *take pride* in serving others and discrediting ourselves. Of course all of that is "flesh" and self-abasement Col 2:18 and is *false humility* where **pride reigns**. But prideful people are headed toward loss and a downfall. Prov.16:18,19 **God opposes the proud but gives grace to the humble**. Prov. 3:34; I Peter 5:5; James 4:6 Pride is all about "me" and seeks honor for myself and from others.

Some say being humble is objectionable, because it would mean that he/she is a reject, fearful or unacceptable. **Not so.** Is humility a fear of explaining/clarifying one's self? **NO.** Is it timidity? **NO.** Because God has not given us a spirit of fear or timidity, but of power and love and discipline. II Tim. 1:7

Some think humility is not expressing an opinion. **Not so.** A humble person expresses his/her wise opinions. Sometimes it is necessary to clarify situations and even to give a clear and firm explanation of one's self, but one does not emotionally rely on being heard, on others agreeing, or on others acceptance and high opinions of one's self. A humble person isn't *defensive* and doesn't force opinions on others. Humble people don't have to accomplish or get accolades for fulfillment and peace, because they know who they are in Christ and who Christ is in them.

> **There is a saying that *humility is not thinking less of yourself, but thinking of yourself less.*** The way we are to think of ourselves is to be based on our union with Christ and His acceptance, protection and provision for us and not on how we in our own strength can find fulfillment and protect ourselves emotionally, etc. In that light, I think the saying is close to the Biblical meaning of humility. In this sense, humility is a sign of Godly strength! It's just the opposite of the world's way. *Dependency on God is necessary for humility.*

> Laying aside our "rights", controls, protections, and dependency on what others think of us and on the things that we believe make us better or more fulfilled, calls for humility. However, if we "try" to lay aside the weight of our fleshly way with its old beliefs and strategies rather than **the focus** being on humility and the mind-set of Christ, it doesn't work! Dependency on the old way is lost as a side-effect when we pursue the new way.

Have you ever thought about this - LACK OF HUMILITY brings forth IMPATIENCE? And impatience exposes ANGER. Whaaat? We try to control life by being passive or aggressive or both. We think we have to have our own way. And we get *impatient* when we can't have our own way! We think we must be in control for things to turn out right for us and others, emotionally and practically. And we feel we need to be right or it degrades us. But LOVE doesn't have to prove it is right, or be in control. I think all of us have been there. When we do go there, we are wrong about how we have approached things, and we need to humble ourselves and APOLOGIZE. Ouch.

Humility is the opposite of pride, haughtiness, self-exaltation, bragging, self-admiration and narcissism. Rather than things being "all about me" - others supporting me, approving me, loving me or recognizing me - I am to *choose* humility. I am to *choose* to *limit myself and my desires in order to put others first*. As *I focus on truth*, my old ways of attempting to find comfort and security, needing to win, to be heard, to be right, needing praise and respect are laid aside.

LOVE is *choosing* humility and service to others. Jesus was referring to the new covenant to come when He said, "But the greatest among you shall be *your servant*. And **whoever exalts himself** shall be **humbled;** and **whoever humbles himself** shall be **exalted**." To be exalted means the person will **be lifted up**. Matt. 23:11-12 In Matt.11:29, Jesus said, "..**learn from Me**, for I am **gentle** and **humble in heart,** and you will find REST for your SOUL**."** Now THAT is an awesome LIFT!

Christ is GOD, and **God** who created all things is a **servant, humble** and **meek** Matt. 11:29 in sacrificing **Himself** *for* others. This **is LOVE**. And we *grow up in Him by doing the same*. If **we humble ourselves** under God, *He* **will lift us up**. This means we will *experience* (know) His grace, joy, peace, provision and protection that is ALREADY ours, and *our soul* - our mind and emotions will be *lifted by Him*. Luke 14:11; 18:14; James 4:10; I Peter 5:6

"He has brought down rulers from *their* thrones, And has exalted those who were **humble**." Luke 1:52 **"Humble yourselves** in the presence of the Lord, and He will **exalt you"**. James 4:10 "Therefore **humble** yourselves under the mighty hand of God, that He may **exalt**

you at the proper time." 1 Peter 5:6   "To sum up, all of you **be** har-monious, sympathetic, brotherly, kindhearted, and **humble** in spirit." 1 Peter 3:18   We are to BE who we already ARE!

We have been equipped by Christ spirit in us to CHOOSE to **clothe ourselves** with **humility** toward one another, because God is opposed to the proud, but He gives grace to the **humble**. Therefore **humble yourselves** under the mighty hand of God, so that He may exalt you at the proper time. 1 Peter 5:5-6

> **Meekness** is **closely associated with humility**. The world does not usually hold **meekness** to be a virtue, because it is seen as weakness or a resignation to be abused or taken advantage of. It is seen as not being assertive. Again, not so! A meek and humble person can be assertive, but in wisdom *limits himself* and his opinions – even if he is right.   He doesn't have to be acknowledged or regarded to be at peace.

Meekness is *choosing* to persevere in an attitude of gentleness toward others even under adverse circumstances, rather than forcing things to go his way. The spiritually meek are confident and strong in God's strength. They reap blessings! Matt. 5:5 Meekness is actually a fruit of the Spirit. Gal. 5:22   We are to **walk in a manner *worthy of our calling,*** with humility, gentleness, patience, showing acceptance of one another *in love*. Eph. 4: 1-2 This can only be achieved *by* the *power* of **LOVE.** 1 Cor.13.

A Servant in Christ is **humble**. Christ came to serve. "..I am among you as the one who serves. Luke 22:27 "...the Son of Man (God) did not come **to BE served**, but **to serve**. Matthew 20:28; Mark 10:45 A humble person *voluntarily chooses* to consider another's needs, inter-ests and opinions – with WISDOM. He takes care of his own interests but considers others more important than himself. This is love. He loves his enemies. *He gives and expects nothing in return.* Luke 6:35

He doesn't look for accolades and for others to reward him by their "being pleased".

We are not to "just please ourselves". Rom. 15:1 "Do not merely look out for own personal interests, but also for the interests of others" Phil. 2:4. This is to be intentional since selfishness is the believer's fleshly way. Love builds up others in faith. Phil. 2:3-4 Love doesn't think highly of his own opinions and performance. Love is respectful but doesn't demand respect. Love doesn't try to get revenge. Rom. 12: 16-18 Love does not seek its own *benefit*. 1 Cor. 13:5 Love *must be* free of hypocrisy. Detest what is evil; cling to what is good. *Be* devoted to one another in brotherly love; GIVE PREFERENCE to ONE ANOTHER in honor, not lagging behind in diligence, fervent in spirit. Rom 12:9-11

The greatest among you is the servant. Matt. 23:11 All of this *works by* love.

> We are to **serve one another *in love*** Gal. 5:13 and SUBMIT ourselves to one another. Eph. 4:2; 5:21 Those who are (or wish to be) leaders or in authority are to humble themselves and serve, PREFERRING others above themselves. Again that great seeming paradox! "...but whoever wishes to become great among you shall be your servant; and whoever wishes to be first among you shall be slave of all.
>
> In the New Testament the Greek word used to refer to a SERVANT is *diakonos*. It means to SERVE another and also means to MINISTER. When we serve others, we are to HUMBLE ourselves, putting them first - before ourselves. This is our ministering to them!

It might be noted here that we don't have to be close friends with someone to LOVE that person. Remember the good Samaritan didn't even know the one to whom he expressed LOVE.

This is when we present ourselves as SLAVES to righteousness. When we love and serve, the world's view of Christianity will change.

It is astounding that HUMILITY is a picture of the Power of God Himself! Now THAT is a MYSTERY to the human, and the worlds, way of understanding.

Therefore, since Christ suffered in his body, ARM YOURSELVES also with THE SAME ATTITUDE. Above all, LOVE each other deeply, because love covers over a multitude of sins. Offer hospitality to one another without grumbling. Each of you should use whatever gift you have received to SERVE others, as faithful stewards of God's grace in its various forms. 1 Peter 4:1,8-10

A mind-set of HUMILITY is necessary as we trust God and let go of reliance on the flesh.

It has been said that the greatest *mark of counterfeit Christianity is lack of humility*. People can serve without humility, but one can not be truly humble without serving. "Whosoever therefore shall humble himself as this little child, the same is greatest in the kingdom of Heaven." Matthew 18:4

"But He gives a greater grace. Therefore *it* says, "God is opposed to the proud, but **gives grace** to the **humble**." James 4:6; 1 Peter 5:5 "Take **My yoke** upon you and **learn from Me**, for I am **gentle and humble** in heart, and you will find **rest** for **your soul**." Matthew 11:29 Our being gentle and humble from the heart breaks away the old fleshly strategies that block our experience of the rest/peace that is ALREADY ours in Him.

We cannot KNOW GOD as He knows us unless we voluntarily take His **YOKE** of **LOVE** – of **HUMILITY**, and servanthood in everything we do, through suffering rejection and persecution. That is the way we learn of Him – learn to KNOW GOD in the POWER of HIS RESURRECTION and in the FELLOWSHIP of HIS SUFFERING. Be confident of His indwelling love and power. Be aware of opportunities to build up, encourage, be diligent to let others experience HIS Life, Light and Love through you.

Can we even imagine that being HUMBLE, a SERVANT, PERFERRING OTHERS above Himself, GIVING HIMSELF UP for the GOOD of others IS the POWER that CREATED ALL things? **That this kind of LOVE IS GOD Himself is almost beyond comprehension**. Phil. 2:3-4; Gal. 2:20; Eph. 5:25

That "low road" of humility **IS** indeed the "highway" of Godliness.

That is LOVE in the Present Tense

CHAPTER 15

P-A-A-TIENCE...

Most of us are impatient at times...

well maybe a lot of the time. Especially if others "tie knots" differently than we do...and we can't seem to get them untied. And it is important that we get them untied as quickly as possible because our, or another's, health, financial security, reputation or contentment depends on it.

Or so we think.

And we can get angry because we believe we can control life. As believers, we know we should trust the Lord as our sufficiency. We know we shouldn't be impatient. Or frustrated. Or fearful. We might say, "Well, I know I *should* be patient, but how important is it really, when I am being treated unfairly, when I don't get what I paid for, etc.?

Okay, think about it. We wouldn't need to BE PATIENT if there weren't adverse situations...

How DO we be patient... When things are so unfair? When our plans are changed and it affects others? When we are hindered in doing something important to us? When we have an urgent health need and meeting it is being blocked? When we are involved with a pro-crastinator? When we give explanations to others to try to get them to understand so things will turn out right, and they don't care or don't comprehend? When we haven't yet gotten what we urgently prayed for? When we fear we will be hurt and we feel we must be in control to validate ourselves or find importance or be secure?

It makes sense to be *impatient* in those circumstances. Doesn't it? To tell the truth, impatience is a result of our *walking after our own understanding*...in the futility of our own mind / thinking. Eph. 4:17, while *walking by the Spirit* is a **mystery**, an enigma, and *opposite of our own human way* with its false beliefs about how to make life work for us.

> Impatience leads to anger which comes from those desires and conflicts that war inside of us. What causes the fights and quarrels among you? Don't they come from your desires that battle within you? James 4:1 NIV Our desires within us are our "own fleshly ways". And, guess what? Love doesn't even seek *its own way/ benefit!* 1 Cor. 13:5

In light of this, have we ever considered that the very situations we get frustrated over may be the specific things we need in order to LEARN patience? I know. That sounds weird. First though, do we re-ally know what the word, *PATIENCE*, means? The New Testament the Greek word for patience is, *hupomone*, and it carries the meaning of **endurance, continuing and being steadfast**. Luke 8;15; 21:19; Rom. 5:3, 15:4 It also indicates to endure under hard times by a decision of one's will and not just out of necessity.

We Believers know that by God's grace we are forgiven, accepted, loved and have been made new creations – complete in Christ. And we have ALREADY been equipped and given all things that pertain to Life and Godliness. BUT do we know that we *experience* more fully those things we ALREADY have, when the **TESTING of our faith** *works* **PATIENCE** (in our soul)? Jas. 1:3

PATIENCE is a fruit of the Spirit. Gal. 5:22   But when we get impatient about the circumstances mentioned above, and our minds are set on finances, security, our reputation, or pleasures of the world, these are "thorns that **choke** the fruit from growing to **maturity"**. Luke 8:14 Remember, He is the vine and we are the branches. And if we abide (by faith *continue, press on*) in Him, we bear much fruit. John 15:5,8

So God prunes the branches by allowing them to *go through trials*, SO THAT they will *learn endurance* and bear MORE fruit. John 15:2 The *pruning* is His *discipline* of allowing us to go through trials and hardships, so we will grow and mature in FAITH expressing itself by LOVE as we face those difficult times, and the result will be others seeing His life in us, which glorifies Him.

PATIENCE is worked out in us as we choose by faith to love, be kind, forgive, serve, put others first, especially **in the face of testing and trials**! Well, what if we have been illegally been taken advantage of or abused? Don't we have a right to be impatient, especially if we are trying to work with others who are incompetent or careless? No... because LOVING in the face of hard times is **when we know Him** in **the power of His resurrection** and **in the fellowship of His suffering.**

The short answer is that impatience hurts US. It interferes with our knowing inner peace and joy. It prevents us from experiencing what is already ours in Christ and the fullness of God's sufficiency. At the same time, we need to know we can choose to grow in love and still draw boundaries while seeking to clarify situations. Does being PATIENT mean we let others continue to take advantage of us without trying to make it right? NO. But we are to endeavor to clarify things and let **ALL** we do be done in **LOVE**. 1 Cor. 16:14

Since patience is translated in scripture as *endurance* or *perseverance*. Love IS **PATIENT** 1 Cor. 13:4…so LOVE perseveres, endures. The *purpose* of our being made new creations, forgiven and without the weight of a self-condemning conscience is SO THAT we can live by faith and let others see Christ revealed through us by our love. This is when we mature in LOVE. This is when we KNOW GOD. Our obedience of faith is to love others. The testing of our faith is our opportunity to choose to persevere - not give up - as we walk in love.

Knowing this, that the trying / ***testing of your faith*** works **PATIENCE**. But let PATIENCE have her perfect work, that ye may be perfect and entire, wanting nothing. James 1: 3-4 NIV Let *perseverance* finish its work so that you may be mature and complete, not lacking anything. This is when we *experience* more fully *(inherit)* the promises (that are ALREADY ours). Heb. 6:12

Being patient and persevering is referred to as a *race we run* as we choose, by His power in us, to grow in our obedience of faith and love for others. Since the fruit of the Spirit is love and PATIENCE, we are to with all humility and gentleness, with **PATIENCE**, show tolerance for one another in love, Eph. 4:2.

It is necessary at this point to REMEMBER that we are ALREADY perfect and complete in our SPIRIT. But we partake, and experience more fully all that is ours in Christ, and we know Him more completely **when we are being transformed and conformed in our human mind – our SOUL - to His likeness and image.** This is Godliness and it only happens through the hard times and persecution we will go through in our lives.

This is when we are growing up to maturity in Christ. It is when **we mature in faith that is expressed by love**. It is when we, by faith, love others and endure in it as we face opposition, testing and trials. We know that loving others - serving them, giving ourselves up for them, not having to prove we are right, showing kindness, etc. - takes a lot of PATIENCE - our allowing His PATIENCE to be exercised in us.

And the result is that we by faith **access** this **grace** wherein we stand. Rom. 5:2 It is when we press on in this obedience of faith that we "**lay hold of** that for which also we were laid **hold of** by Christ Jesus" Phil. 3:12 which is to experience our salvation - eternal Life - not just in the hereafter but also in this present world – *when we are revealed with Him in His glory for others to see.*

In other words, faith expresses itself by LOVE. Gal. 5:6 And LOVE IS PATIENT. Love is the *evidence* and *proof* of our faith and His indwelling us that others need to experience. "Wherefore seeing we also are compassed about with so great a cloud of witnesses, let us lay aside every weight, and the sin which doth so easily beset us, and let us run with **PATIENCE** (endurance NASB / perseverance NIV) the race (our persevering in faith and love) that is set before us. Heb. (KJV)

Don't give up when our faith is tested by situations such as were mentioned above!

PATIENCE is when *we discipline ourselves* in this *obedience of faith* – especially when we are hindered in some way. And **the purpose is for godliness to be revealed through us.** 1 Tim 4: 7-8 It is to set one's mind on the spirit – the attitude of Christ (Love). It is to *persevere in our work of faith and labor of love.* 1 Thess. 1:3 It is then that our faith is proved to others by our love. We cannot grow to maturity without allowing PATIENCE to be worked in and through us.

Growing to maturity, being conformed to His image, being made perfect (mature, complete) in our human mind/soul just as we ARE already perfect and complete in spirit, is **God's *intention* for us**. It happens as we exercise faith to love others especially when we are tested and must choose to patiently endure / persevere / not give up in this walk of faith. This is when Christ will be revealed in and thru us for others to see, and is God's purpose for His creations - His children - as they walk on this earth.

For what credit is there if, when you sin and are harshly treated, you endure it with patience? But if when you do what is right (i.e. love others) and suffer for it and you PATIENTLY endure it, this finds favor with God. 1 Peter 2:20   So we are not to be spiritually sluggish (lazy), but imitators of those who through **faith** and **patience** **inherit the promises**. Heb. 6:12

We are to, as Paul did, be servants of God, in much endurance, in afflictions, in hardships, in distresses, in purity, in knowledge, in **PATIENCE,** in kindness, in the Holy Spirit, in genuine love, [7] in the word of truth, in the power of God. (2 Cor.6: 4, 6,7)

> We urge you, brethren, admonish the unruly, encourage the fainthearted, help the weak, be **PATIENT** with everyone. 1 Thess. 5:14 The Lord's bond-servant must not be quarrelsome, but be kind to all, able to teach, **PATIENT** when wronged . 2 Tim. 2:24 So, as those who have been chosen of God, holy and beloved, put on a heart of compassion, kindness, humility, gentleness and **PATIENCE**. Col.3:12

Love is **PATIENT**, love is kind and is not jealous; love does not brag and is not arrogant, does not act unbecomingly; it does *not seek its own*, is not provoked, does not take into account a wrong suffered. 1 Cor. 13: 4-5   Love is a choice to have the inner attitude of a servant and walk in love, *just as* Christ also **loved** us and **gave Himself up** for us, *an offering and a sacrifice to God as a fragrant aroma*. Eph. 5:2 This is our obedience of faith – our work of faith**.**

So the testing of our faith works outwardly the fruit of Christ's spirit that indwells us. And the fruit of the Spirit is love, joy, peace, **PATIENCE**, kindness, goodness, faithfulness. Patience is far more important than we might have thought.

It is likely that we haven't heard, or thought much of, how important PATIENCE is in walking after the Spirit in our relationships. As PATIENCE is worked in us, we grow up in Christ. We are to no longer be children in Him. But remember that as babies, children, and youth grow and run this race of faith, they will fall down and get hurt sometimes, but they get back up and persevere to maturity, the goal.

Through it all, we are to speak the truth in love, and **grow up** in all aspects into Him who is the head, even Christ. Eph. 4:15 And we will be *strengthened* with all power, according to His glorious might, for the attaining of all steadfastness and patience; joyously giving thanks to the Father, who has **qualified us** to share in the inheritance of the saints in Light. Col. 1: 11-12

We have addressed different aspects of LOVE being HUMILITY and PATIENCE. But did we know...DISCIPLINE is also involved in our expressing Love?

That is LOVE in the Present Tense

CHAPTER 16

Discipline? But Why?

We often think of DISCIPLINE

as harsh or rough treatment, or inflicting pain or loss on a person because of their wrong doing... or a person getting what he/she deserves - "getting justice" - for wrongs he/she committed. BUT what does the word, DISCIPLINE really MEAN in New Testament Greek? What is the difference in the words, "discipline", "punishment", and "chasten"? These words MAY NOT MEAN what most people think!

The word DISCIPLINE as used in the New Covenant scriptures in this writing and in NT Greek is *paideia*, which means EDUCATION or training. And CHASTEN means much the same thing, as in the Greek, *paideuo* is to train up a child, i.e. EDUCATE, INSTRUCT, LEARN, teach. These words do NOT refer to "punishment" which in Greek is *kolazo,* and means inflicting a penalty for sin.

There are ***intense*** exhortations to believers who are **already new creations** in Christ, unconditionally and totally accepted, forgiven of past, present and future sins, born of His Spirit and forever joined as one with Him – to DISCIPLINE THEMSELVES. We are also told BECAUSE we are His children, our Father GOD DISCIPLINES us. Heb. 12:7 DISCIPLINE for Believers? But ...WHY?

We are told to **discipline ourselves** for the **purpose of godliness,** for *bodily* discipline is only of little profit, but GODLINESS is profitable for all things, since it holds PROMISE for the PRESENT LIFE and *also for the life to come.* It is a trustworthy statement deserving full acceptance. 1 Tim 4:7-9 GODLINESS. Really?

God disciplines us and we are to **discipline ourselves** for our *obedience of faith.* For the GRACE of God has appeared, bringing salvation to all men, INSTRUCTING us to ***deny ungodliness*** and worldly desires and to live sensibly, righteously and godly in the PRESENT AGE. Titus 2:11-12 And by the power of the Holy Spirit, the written Word teaches us, reproves and corrects us, and **trains us** in ***righteousness*** so that we, *the people of God* may be ADEQUATE, EQUIPPED for every GOOD WORK. 2 Tim. 3:16-17

The reason God DISCIPLINES us IS NOT for God to give us what we deserve because we have sinned or failed, because Christ Himself bore our sins in His body on the cross. He offered one sacrifice for sins for all time 1 Peter 2:24; Heb. 10:12   And we ARE NOT told to *discipline ourselves* to *obey religious LAW,* because Christ fulfilled the law on behalf of believers. He said, "Do not think that I came to abolish the Law or the Prophets; I did not come to abolish but to fulfill. Matt. 5:17

Okay.

If we are not under law, but are under Grace, new creations with the Life and Likeness of Christ indwelling our new spirit, and God has ALREADY granted us ALL things pertaining to Life and Godliness through the knowledge of Him 1 Peter 1:3, WHY would we DISCIPLINE ourselves - or WHY would God discipline us *for the purpose of Godliness*?   And HOW?

The word GODLINESS as in New Covenant Greek, is from the words *eusebeia* and *sebomai* which together mean to REVERE or **WORSHIP BY** being resolute and **standing firm in faith** focusing on who God is - in us and for us - and as a result, living out His inner LIKENESS.

The LIKENESS of God lives within a believer's **spirit,** and it is the attitude of Christ - of LOVE - humility, patience, kindness, forgiveness, being a servant, giving Himself up for others. And as has been stated in former chapters, we are told to "be **renewed** in the spirit of **our (human) mind** - to PUT ON our NEW SELF - which in the LIKENESS of God *has been created* in righteousness and holiness of the truth." Eph. 4:24 "Putting on the new self" is to be conformed in one's human mind/attitude to Christ's LIKENESS that lives in our spirit - and living it out.

This is one's being CONFORMED to GODLINESS. And this is the PURPOSE of our DISCIPLINE. It is our being transformed (to His likeness) by the renewing of our mind. Rom. 12:2. 1 Tim. 6:3-4 says If anyone advocates a different doctrine and does not agree with sound words, those of Christ, and with the doctrine *conforming to Godliness*, he is conceited and understands nothing; but he has a morbid interest in controversial questions and disputes about words, out of which arise envy, strife, abusive language, evil suspicions.

SO what might *prompt us* or "goad us" to put on our new self – the image – the likeness /mind of Christ? Col. 3:10,12,14   The HARD TIMES that come to all humans can nudge us to do that. We are encouraged to: ENDURE HARDSHIP as DISCIPLINE (teaching / education); because God is treating you as his children. For what children are not disciplined by their father? If you are not disciplined - and everyone undergoes discipline - then you are not legitimate, not true sons and daughters at all. Heb. 12:6-8 NIV

We are told that God DISCIPLINES us for OUR GOOD, in order that we may SHARE in His HOLINESS. At the time, all **discipline** seems a cause not for joy but for pain, yet **later it brings** the peaceful **fruit of righteousness** to those who are *trained by it*. Heb. 12:10-11

This is so that we might EXPERIENCE and LIVE OUT what we ALREADY have and BE who we ALREADY ARE, and so Christ will BE REVEALED through us for others to see. No discipline seems pleasant at the time, but painful. Later on, however, it produces a HARVEST of RIGHTEOUSNESS and PEACE for those who have **been trained** by it. Heb. 12:1-2; 5-11 NIV   And it is when Christ, who is our life, is REVEALED, then you also will be REVEALED with Him in (His) glory. Col. 3:4

So we now see **God's Purpose** in **discipline** and allowing hard times - trials and adversity – in the lives of those who belong to Him. But did we know that ENDURANCE is involved in all aspects of LOVE?

That is LOVE in The Present Tense

CHAPTER 17

What Does Endurance Have to Do With It?

It is absolutely SO difficult

when we are "crucified" by others. When we experience an untimely loss of a loved one. When we lose our job and can't find another one. When we grieve. When we fear. When we hurt. When we are rejected or abandoned by others. Have you ever had someone to make assumptions about you and lie to others about you, and you later realize they misrepresented you and others are shunning you?

Sometimes we think that Godliness and loving others shouldn't involve suffering, pain or persecution. But if we are to **KNOW** Christ, we must know Him and the **power of His resurrection** AND the **fellowship of His sufferings**, being **conformed** to **His death**. Phil. 3:9-11 We are told that all who DESIRE to LIVE GODLY in Christ Jesus will be PERSECUTED. 2 Tim. 3:12

The early church was urged **to not be surprised** at the FIERY ORDEAL that has come on you to test you, as though something strange were happening to you. But rejoice inasmuch as you *participate in the* *sufferings* of Christ, SO THAT you may be overjoyed when his glory is revealed. 1 Peter 4:12-13 NIV

Therefore, **prepare your minds for action**, keep sober *in spirit*, **fix** your hope completely on the grace to be brought to you at the revelation of Jesus Christ. 1 Peter 1:13

> The process of learning to ENDURE / persevere through trials with Christ's mind-set is the process by which we come to KNOW HIM in the power of His resurrection and the fellowship of His sufferings, being conformed to His death.

God is not the author of sin and evil, but He uses the evil and tribulations that are in the present world so that we will learn (discipline ourselves) to grow in our work of expressing faith by LOVE. It is then that we partake more fully of what is ALREADY ours in Him. Remember that God causes all things to work together **for good** to those who love God, to those who are called according to *His* purpose. Rom. 8:28-29   Trials will come to ALL, but those who are not born of God's Spirit don't have the Power to endure and overcome through the Hard Times and victoriously abide in His peace, grace, joy and righteousness.

In everything commending ourselves as servants of God, in much **ENDURANCE**, in AFFLICTIONS, in HARDSHIPS, in DISTRESSES. 2 Cor. 6:4 For you have need of ENDURANCE, so that when you have done the will of God, you may receive what was promised. Heb. 10:36 Therefore, since we have so great a cloud of witnesses surrounding us, **let us also lay aside every encumbrance and the sin which so easily entangles us,** and let us **run with ENDURANCE the race** that is set before us. Heb. 12:1 Know that the TESTING OF YOUR FAITH *produces* ENDURANCE.

And let ENDURANCE have *its* perfect result, *so that you may be perfect and complete, lacking in nothing*. James 1:3-4 This means so the fruit of the spirit (the Vine) will grow and mature. This is when we *mature in Faith*.

We are to ENDURE until we all attain to the unity of the faith, and of the KNOWLEDGE of the SON of GOD, to a **mature** man, to the measure of the stature which belongs to the **fullness of Christ**. Eph. 4:13

> The Apostle Paul said he was rejoicing to see the believers' good DISCIPLINE and the STABILITY OF their FAITH in Christ. Col. 2:5 They had to discipline themselves by reminding and educating themselves further in the truth and to **choose** for it to *continually* be their focus. This is to **ENDURE**. This led to their pressing on and standing more firmly in expressing their faith through **LOVE** - which is to live out His LIKENESS of humility, being a servant, and giving themselves up for others.

Sometimes we think our enduring in faith or exercising our faith means to trust God to meet our needs, deliver us and carry us safely through hard times. YES that is the foundation, but based on that, we must *go further* and exercise our FAITH to express itself through LOVE, which is the *only thing* that counts. Gal. 5:6 And this is when we KNOW God. 1 John 4:7

Our KNOWING God is experiencing Eternal Life. John 17:3   It can happen now in this present world when we choose to PRESS ON and ENDURE in FAITH with our eyes focused on Him, the Truth, the Life, and Peace. His divine power has granted to us everything pertaining to Life and Godliness, *through* the true KNOWLEDGE of Him who called us by His own glory and excellence. 1 Peter 1:2-3

We are to **suffer hardship** as good **soldiers** of Christ Jesus. 2 Tim. 2:3 All DISCIPLINE for the moment seems not to be joyful, but sorrowful; yet to those who have been TRAINED by it, *afterwards* it YIELDS the peaceful FRUIT of righteousness Heb. 12:11 that is, the fruit of the Spirit. Christ in us is our strength to do these things. He said, I am the vine, you are the branches; he who ABIDES in Me and I in him, he bears much fruit, for apart from Me you can do nothing.

To ABIDE is not passivity, but it means "to continue" to **ENDURE**, to PRESS ON and STAND FIRM in EXERCISING FAITH to express LOVE - His Life - so others may see His glory and desire to also KNOW Him. 1 Cor.15:58; 16:13; Gal. 5:1, 1 Thess. 3:8, Eph. 6:11,13; 2 Peter 3:17 Col. 1:23

Therefore, beloved, since you look for these things, be DILIGENT to be FOUND by HIM in PEACE, SPOTLESS and BLAMELESS. Be on your guard so that you are not carried away by the error of unprincipled men and *fall from your own STEADFASTNESS*, but GROW in the GRACE and KNOWLEDGE of our Lord and Savior Jesus Christ. To Him *be* the glory, both now and to the day of eternity. Amen. 2 Peter 3: 14,18

If we DO stumble and fall on the way, God doesn't condemn us. *If we feel condemned, we do it to ourselves. We condemn ourselves!* So stand back up and continue the race of faith.

We are to LIVE OUT our GODLINESS...Discipline ourselves for the PURPOSE OF GODLINESS; for bodily discipline is only of little profit, but GODLINESS is profitable for all things, since it holds PROMISE for the PRESENT LIFE and *also* for THE LIFE TO COME. It is a trustworthy statement deserving full acceptance. For it is for this we **labor and strive**, because we have fixed our hope on the living God, who is the Savior of all men, especially of believers. 1 Tim 4:7-10 Here to labor and strive indicates their pressing on in faith.

The word, ***strive*** in Greek has several different meanings that can range from being antagonistic and quarreling - to **enduring** - *which* *is the meaning spoken of here.* Phil. 1:27-29 NIV speaks of **striving together for the faith** of the gospel, which means to **press on** and **endure** in faith without being frightened in any way by those who oppose you. This is *a sign to them* that they will be destroyed, but that you will be saved—and that by God. For it has been granted to you on behalf of Christ not only to believe in him, but also to suffer for Him.

We must ENDURE in FAITH **so that** our **faith will not be in vain**. Phil. 2:16 *In Vain* **means that the intended goal isn't reached.** Prescribe and teach these things. Let no one look down on your youthfulness, but rather in speech, conduct, love, faith *and* purity, **show yourself** an **example** of those who believe. 1 Tim. 4:7-11

Or am I striving to please men? If I were still trying to please men, I would not be a bond-servant of Christ. Gal. 1:10 Only CONDUCT YOURSELVES in a manner worthy of the gospel of Christ, so that whether I come and see you or remain absent, I will hear of you that you are standing firm in one spirit, with one mind **striving** (enduring) together for the **faith** of the gospel. Phil. 1:27 We proclaim Him, admonishing every man and teaching every man with all wisdom, so that we may present every man *complete in Christ.*

For this purpose also I labor, STRIVING according to His power, which mightily works within me. Col. 1:28-29 Knowing that I am **strengthened with all power**, according to His glorious might, for the attaining of all PERSEVERANCE and PATIENCE; joyously. Col. 1:11

Remember, the purpose of our STRIVING / ENDURING in FAITH is NOT to earn anything from God, because we ALREADY have been joined with Him forever, are totally loved and accepted by Him, and have been given all things pertaining to LIFE and Godliness. But as we are seeing here, our living out our LIFE in Christ does not happen automatically. It is not being passive. Rather, it is to intentionally be STEADFAST.

Do not believe in vain. ENDURE. Don't FALL AWAY from your STEADFASTNESS. For if we go on sinning willfully after receiving the knowledge of the truth, there no longer remains a sacrifice for sins. 1 Cor. 15:2; 15:58, Heb. 10:26   This means that if we go on sinning after we believe, Christ's sacrifice for us becomes of NO EFFECT for us individually *in our present INNER experience*. It doesn't mean we fall from our eternal union with God. It means we fall from our EXPERIENCE of knowing Him more fully and His Kingdom of righteousness, peace and joy here in the present time.

Here we have seen that it is by **HARD TIMES** and *discipline* that we learn to ***develop patience and endurance.*** The testing of our faith is the opportunity for patience and all of the other fruit of the Spirit to grow to maturity in us. In other words, so **that in our soul** we may be perfect and complete (mature) as we already are in our spirit - lacking in nothing (as the LIFE of Christ is appropriated / experienced by us in our soul.) James. 1:4

That is LOVE in The Present Tense.

CHAPTER 18

Get Ready for the Hard Times. Be a Prepper.

Can there actually be a *purpose* in hard times -

the trials and adversity believers go through? Could they be related to **our maturing** in Christ? Could a reason be related to our walking after the flesh – after our old left-over worldly lusts, beliefs and behaviors? Why? Could there be a "divine design" woven into it all?

We don't easily turn loose of our familiar and often good-looking fleshly patterns, which *BLOCK* our *laying hold more completely* on the Life, Freedom and good gifts that *already* dwell in our spirit as believers.

Our hard times can be fiery at times. And unfair. At times, maybe we even feel we are in a type of war. And we believe the battle is with other people. And we struggle to fight the enemy with our old ineffective ways. But Eph. 6:12 tells us that *our struggle is not against flesh and blood*, but against the rulers, against the powers, against the world forces of this darkness, against the spiritual *forces* of wickedness in the heavenly places.

There are those in Christ who are praying "hedges of protection" in every valley so that "nothing shall by any means harm" them and so they won't "dash their foot against a stone", but instead, they experience calamities. And it isn't working. Others believe they must try to do everything perfectly according to religious "rules" to avoid pain and suffering. And it isn't working.

Hard times come to ALL regardless of the cause.

People often wonder why some Godly minister or other saintly person endures illness, persecution, or loss when it is evident that he/she is a believer and has by faith received God's forgiveness and trusts the indwelling Christ. How many times have we heard these questions, "Why is this horrible thing happening to me? I've been close to God and am just as good as the next person. If God is a loving God, why would He allow such bad things to happen to me and my loved ones?"

Some of us, in an attempt to answer this for ourselves, will have intense guilt or resentment as we become introspective and focus on the past or on what we, or another person, did or did not do to bring about the adversity. On the other hand, religious people may say, "The devil is really after me," or "I guess I forgot to put my armor on this morning," or "maybe I should have fasted and prayed more." Or "I exercised faith in God's grace and His protection, but the tornado hit us anyway." Or we might just become angry with God.

Could it really be….?

Trials and adversity come to all people, and scripture tells us these hard times happen to believers and non-believers alike. But we have difficulty understanding that injustice, unfairness, grief, and distress are allowed by God for a purpose, whether these things happen as a consequence of something we have done – or not. Our "hard times" can even be small repeated everyday frustrations hindrances.

And it is hard to comprehend that God would ORCHESTRATE these difficult times together with all other circumstances in the lives of those who love Him so the result would be for their good and His glory. **Could that really be true?**

Could it be?

Could it be that we are trying to avoid the very tools the Lord would use to bring us into his best, to even conform us to His image? This is a huge matter for us to consider – and understand.

A sweet young lady, who is a believer, said to me, "I have heard the message that believers can expect to have hard times and trials, but it makes me depressed to think about it…"   She had not yet begun to realize there is a way to face unfairness and adversity that could lead her to experience freedom from depression and to the enjoyment of blessings she never expected.

Natural occurrences can become the tools God uses in one's life. It might be illnesses, financial loss, or death of a loved one. It could be persecution and loss of reputation because of someone's jealousy, or even the consequences of one's own behavior. OR adversity might be an attack by the powers of darkness. There are any number of various adversities in life. They can be large or small afflictions of body or mind. *But whatever hard time we encounter is perfectly suited to loosen our grip on a specific area of our living according to our fleshly ways and not by His Spirit and power in us.*

We are told that all who desire to be Godly will suffer persecution. 2 Tim. 3:12 REALLY? Not many would think that. And there is a reason for those Hard Times.

Yes. It's another MYSTERY.

Now imagine this. We can be so attached to our fleshly ways (those self-centered beliefs and behaviors) that, in the grand scheme of life, God allows among other things, the unique personalities and the actions of *certain people to become some of the specific instruments He works together in an omniscient design to break our hold on our personal style of ineffective flesh!* **Their ways can be reciprocal to our ways**. *And their ways can become our hard times* – our trials. Wow.

This is a very simple example. Early in life I developed a belief that "I must not be misunderstood". It was only one of the beliefs that made up the "weight in my baggage". I learned later that my fear of life going wrong for myself and others, and a fear of rejection was behind it. It was behind other beliefs such as, "I must try hard to clarify myself and must be emotionally guarded to stay safe". At the same time, that led to my arguing to prove my point with certain people and avoiding being open around others.

So what has happened over and over in my life? My actions and my words being misunderstood. And the pain that came with it. God has allowed the natural occurrence of the hurt of being misunderstood, criticized, shunned and rejected as His instruments - His goads - to frustrate me to focus on the truth that HE is my security and protection and to respond with the mind of Christ. I had to be willing to be perceived as wrong or even guilty at times – when I wasn't – and trust Him to be my Peace.

It has been a process, but in it a lot of fleshly beliefs and strategies that blocked my experiencing His life more fully have been broken away and my desire is that I am growing stronger, **maturing** (being perfected) **in faith** with the attitude of Christ. And in it all, I am hopefully learning to LOVE others who were involved in the painful circumstances.

Remember that Christ in us is a light to the world, and ***our old familiar*** *false beliefs and strategies can be like a woven basket placed over a lighted candle. It blocks the light within from entirely shining through.* The adversity God allows to come our way can be the very thing we need to abandon the old ways that hinder us and others from experiencing Christ in us more completely.

There is a reason. For the Hard Times.

We are persecuted, but not forsaken; struck down, but not destroyed; always carrying about in the body the dying of Jesus so the LIFE of JESUS also may be REVEALED IN our BODY. For we who live are *constantly being handed over to death* because of Jesus' **so that** the LIFE OF JESUS also may also BE REVEALED IN our MORTAL FLESH. 2 Cor. 4:9-11 This is *proof of our faith to others* to see and experience – God's high calling for us. 1 Peter 1:6-8; Phil. 2:15

This speaks a bit of how God *in His sovereignty* works *all things together* for good for those who love Him and are called according to His purpose. Rom. 8:28 Okay. So God uses **trials and adversity as opportunities for us to abandon walking in ways that prevent us and others from experiencing** the fullness **of** His Life in us.

AND that isn't all.

As we understand how **LOVE** is expressed through *humility, patience* and *endurance*, we can begin to see the PURPOSE of HARD TIMES. **The purpose of our faith** being **tested by trials** is that it is the *opportunity* **for us to choose** that the **mind of Christ,** which is to serve others by Love - humility, patience and endurance - would be the focus of our human mind and experience.

It is so that you will not be sluggish, but imitators of those who through *faith* and *patience* *inherit the promises.* Heb.6:12 This is when we *enjoy* to a greater degree the good things in Christ that are ALREADY ours. And it is when we **know Him** and the **power of His resurrection** and the **fellowship of His sufferings**, being **conformed** to His death. Phil. 3:10

Consider it all joy, my brethren, when you encounter various trials, knowing that the testing of your faith produces endurance. *And let **endurance** have its perfect result, **so that you may be perfect and complete***, *lacking in nothing*. Yes. We are ALREADY perfect and complete in Christ but hard times can be what is needed for us to lay hold on and experience what is ALREADY ours!

After you have suffered for a little while, the God of all grace, who called you to His eternal glory in Christ, will Himself perfect, confirm, strengthen, *and* establish *you*. 1 Peter 5:10

When our faith endures and expresses itself by **LOVE** (Gal. 5:6) in the face of Hard Times, it is when we **know him** and the **power of his resurrection** and the **fellowship** of **his sufferings,** being **conformed** to **his death.** Phil. 3:10 It is God's high calling for His people. It is our intimacy with God.

There is More...

In 1 Peter 4: 12-17, believers are told **not to be surprised** that a fiery ordeal or hard time comes, as if some strange thing were happening to them, because *it's purpose is to test them*. The test is to *reveal who they are* and *if they are walking after the Spirit*.

2 Thessalonians 1:4-5 calls adversities and persecutions a clear indication of **the righteous judgment of God**. Here *judgment* means the trial is a test or process that brings to light whether believers will respond by walking after the Spirit and Truth OR if they will harden

their heart, resist yielding to God, and willfully continue after the fleshly mind-set and behaviors. When we harden our heart and resist the Hard Times by our flesh and the world's ways, *our response backfires on us*!

The test or trial is *a judgment* in the sense that our response to it *can reveal Christ through us, **showing and proving to others that we have been born of God and made worthy by Him*** for His kingdom. Here, being worthy doesn't mean our earning or deserving to partake of the righteousness, joy, and peace of God's Kingdom. Eph. 4:1-3

Scripture tells us that trials and adversity **will happen to all** people, and are a judgment of all, both those who are alive in Christ and those who are dead in sin. 1 Peter 5:9, 4:17   But it begins with His household of faith - with believers. The trials and hard times are *God's discipline and training in our lives to unveil Christ in us and bring us to a place of experiencing His Life and the promises He has already given us*. Heb.12:4-8, 1 Cor.11:32

And it is believers who are equipped to respond and overcome in the face of adversity with the *result* being to *our benefit* and *God's glory.*

So we struggle. And it is warfare. But 2 Cor. 10:4 lets us know that *the weapons of our warfare* are not of flesh (meaning not things of the visible world), but are divinely powerful for the destruction of fortresses (in the spiritual realm). God has GIVEN US the ARMOR we need to fight these spiritual battles. And since our struggle in the hard times *is spiritual*, we must be equipped with *spiritual armor.*

Therefore, **prepare** your **minds** for **action**, keep sober *in spirit*, set your hope completely on the grace to be brought to you at the revelation of Jesus Christ. 1 Peter 1:13

Since we know that **all who desire to be Godly will suffer persecution,**

2 Tim. 3:12 there are things we need to know to **prepare our minds** for this. We need to **be *preppers.***

So Arm Yourselves!

At the beginning of 1 Peter 4, the believers are encouraged **to *arm themselves.*** It says, …as Christ hath suffered for us in the flesh, **ARM YOURSELVES** likewise with the **SAME MIND**. KJV The reason they need to be armed is so they will be prepared and protected *when the trial comes*. And so they will live out the will of God. *What kind of armor* was Peter talking about?

The **ARMOR is** Christ's mind-set of **LOVE,** which is the focus of this book. "Arming ourselves" is again another way of saying the same thing. It is of course INNER armor. It is spiritual armor for spiritual protection. ***It is to arm one's self with the same mind-set that Christ had when He lived and suffered for us.*** It is His attitude of LOVE that is to be lived out in the midst of trials by humility, patience, discipline and endurance.

Consider it **all joy**, my brothers *and sisters*, **when you encounter various trials**, knowing that the testing of your faith produces ENDURANCE. Since we have addressed endurance in preceding chapters, be reminded to let endurance have *its* perfect result, **so that you may be perfect and complete,** lacking in nothing. James 1:2-4 After you have suffered for a little while, the God of all grace, who called you to His eternal glory in Christ, will Himself perfect, confirm, strengthen, *and* establish *you*. 1 Peter 5:10

For what credit is there if, when you **sin** and are *harshly treated*, you endure it with patience? But if when you do **what is right** and **suffer for it you patiently endure** it, this finds favor with God. For you have been **called for this purpose**, since Christ also *suffered for you*, leaving you **an example** for you to follow in His steps. 1 Peter 2:20 He

LOVED others as He endured persecution. If we are to KNOW HIM in the power of His resurrection, we must **also walk in the fellowship of His suffering, being conformed to His death.** Phil. 3:10

Therefore, since Christ has suffered in the flesh, ARM YOURSELVES also with the SAME PURPOSE, because he who has suffered in the flesh has ceased from sin, so as to live the rest of the time in the flesh (the mortal body) no longer for the lusts of men, but for the will of God. 1 Peter 4:1-2 Therefore let us lay aside (abandon) the deeds **of** darkness and put on the **armor of light**. Rom. 13:12

In other words**, our armor is to discipline ourselves to walk by faith expressing itself by Love** – especially through times of suffering.

And during oppositions and persecutions we are to press on and endure in faith and LOVE without being frightened in any way by those who oppose us. This is *a sign to them* that they will be destroyed, but that we will be saved—and that by God. For it has been *granted to us on behalf of Christ not only to believe in him, but also to suffer for Him.* Phil. 1:27-29

> Be encouraged to *continue in the faith*, because it is through *many tribulations* we must enter the kingdom of God, which means to lay hold on and experience the eternal life that is within us.

In this you greatly rejoice, even though now for a little while, if necessary, you have been distressed by various trials, that the **proof of your faith**, being more precious than gold which is perishable, even though tested by fire, **may be found to result in praise and glory and honor at the revelation of Jesus Christ."** 1 Peter 1:7

When He is being revealed in and through us shows that we are *being conformed in our soul to His image that is in our spirit.* **Being conformed to His image and likeness is our very calling and His will for** *us.* It happens as He is working all things together for good for those who love Him and are called according to His purpose. Rom. 8:29

Now we know to be prepared for the trials that WILL come and wh we will need to endure. So be a Prepper!

A Reminder of the Purpose of Trials:

- **That we *would be conformed* to Christ's image.** Rom. 8:29 His image is His mind-set. Phil. 2:5-8

- **That the *life of Christ may be manifest (revealed) in our mortal body.* II Cor. 4:11; Rom. 12:2**

- **That we would *Know Him* in the fellowship of His suffering and in the power of His resurrection -** which is to know more intimately His Life, rather than the destructive fruit of our "own way" - now in this present world. Phil. 3:10; John 17:3; I John 5:20; I Tim. 6:12

- ***That we would bear much fruit* of the Spirit and *glorify* God** John 15:8; Rom. 7:4

- ***That we would experience more completely* the *promises of righteousness, peace and joy that are already ours in Christ.*** Rom. 14:17

- ***That we would be perfected in love.*** 1 John 4: 16-18

- ***Be free of anxiety and fear*** I Peter 5: 6,7   Perfect love (maturing love, humility) casts out fear . I John 4:18

- ***Love one another***   John 15:17

All of these concepts overlap and **they ALL mean the SAME thing**: to *humble* ourselves, to *love*, to *obey*, to *mature* in Him. It is *to abide*. It is to *worship* God. This is the *work of faith* - the faith that expresses itself by love. James 2: 17-18, 26; Gal. 5:6 It is to remove the bushel from over the light within. It is to be Christ's disciple.

That is LOVE in The Present Tense

CHAPTER 19

Out of the Heart the Mouth Speaks

**As we ENDURE in Faith expressing itself
by LOVE through Trials and Hard Times**

we mature in Christ and are being conformed to His likeness by the renewing of our mind (the purifying our heart). **This is proof of our faith.**

And there is no greater indicator of our mind-set and the condition of our heart than the words we speak on a consistent basis. Out of the abundance of the heart the mouth speaks. Luke 6:45 But we may be left wondering just what a humble heart - the *mind of a servant* - is *supposed to actually think about* as we go through the hours of each day - raising our kids, working at our job, being informed on current events.....and well yes...golfing.

> We are urged to choose to **dwell on** the truths of *Christ's Mind-set* of *Love* for us and in us – and whatever is **true**, whatever is **honorable**, whatever is **right**, whatever is **pure**, whatever is **lovely**, whatever is of **good repute**, things that are **excellent** and things **worthy of praise**. Phil. 4: 8-9

But this seems impossible! When we are considering our relationships with family, friends, co-workers and acquaintances, and the political climate, a lot of what is going on **is not** pure, a good report, lovely and so on… So what are we to do? Are we to ignore the facts and not talk about these things? Are we not to be informed? Are we not supposed to verbalize our "take" on things…not give our opinions regarding problems that arise?

We must keep in mind that this is a growing process, and after a while of intentionally focusing on Christ's mind-set as in Phil. 2:5-8, these truths can become sub-conscious, and will come forth as we encounter various testings and difficulties. As we continue to **remind ourselves of what the mind of Christ is (His *likeness* and *image*) and prepare ourselves to respond with that attitude**, it will eventually come to our awareness more often when we face ordinary times, a stressful situation, an argument….or even on the golf course.

I recently heard a believer who knew his identity as a new creation in Christ say that the best way to control our speech is to keep our mind filled with the truth about who we already are in Christ. Well. It is awesome to know who we are in Him. BUT. As we have seen, we are to **dwell on** the MIND-SET / ATTITUDE of Christ who indwells us and not on our identity. Jesus knew who He was and didn't use that to His own advantage!

When I told an acquaintance that I was thinking of writing about the power of our words, he retorted, "I do not believe that God wants us to go around being worried about everything we say!" Well, he was right…we aren't supposed to worry about it! We are not to be *focused on* controlling *outer behaviors* such as the words we speak!

WE are to be DILIGENT in FOCUSING on TRUTH and PUTTING ON the MIND-SET - *the likeness* - of Christ in our human mind, and what we say **will result.** Yes, and after times of "blowing it", we just re-set our focus and continue.

We don't have to go around "gritting our teeth" worrying about what we say. The things that proceed **out of the mouth** come from **the heart / mind**, and those are the things *(in the heart / mind)* that **defile** the person! Matt. 12:34; 15:18; Luke 6:45   So that is a reason to be diligent about maturing or being transformed in our mind - our heart - to His likeness. The issues of life **flow out of it**. Prov. 4:23) And they flow out through our mouth **revealing** what is in our heart!

> The good man out of his good treasure *(the mind-set of Christ in us)* brings forth what is good; and the evil man out of his evil treasure brings forth what is evil. And I say unto you that every careless word that men shall speak, they shall render account for it in the day of judgment. For by your words you shall be justified and by your words you shall be condemned. Matt.12:35-37 In other words, God doesn't condemn us, but **WE will condemn *ourselves - our own heart / mind* - by our words!**

Therefore, do not throw away your confidence, which has a great reward. For you have need of **endurance**, so that when you have done the will of God, you may receive what was promised.   Heb. 10: 35-36

We aren't to *worry* about the words we should speak, but in our **heart** we are to **STUDY HOW to answer.**   Prov. 15:28 Our conversation with others should be based on truth. Not just facts. Jesus is truth. *And remember that all facts are not truth!* Our response is to be based on things that are honorable meaning respectful and proper. Our words are to reflect what is right, pure, lovely and commendable, gracious, holy, spiritually attractive and so on.

Our speaking should always be with grace as if it were seasoned with salt...not dry and flat...but meaningful, building up others and being gentle toward them. Col. 4:5-7 We are to esteem others better than ourselves. The heart of those who are growing in Christ must **PATIENTLY CONSIDER how to answer, be quick to listen but slow to speak**. Prov. 15:28; James 1:19

All of this was spoken to believers under the New Covenant of Grace and Love. They were told, "Let no unwholesome word proceed from your mouth, but **only such a word as is good for edification** (building others up in love) according to the need of the moment, *so that it will give grace to those who hear*. Do NOT GRIEVE the HOLY SPIRIT of God, by whom you were sealed (*forever*) for the day of redemption." Eph. 4:29-30

We must remind ourselves to **do all things without complaining or arguments so** that we will **prove ourselves to be** blameless and innocent, **children of God** above reproach in the midst of a crooked and perverse generation, among whom we appear as lights in the world.

A word fitly spoken is like apples of gold in pictures of silver.   Prov. 25:11

Just *What* Flows Out?

Out of the abundance of the heart, the mouth speaks. Matthew 12:34

To help *test our heart* to see if we are walking in the faith and growing toward maturity II Cor. 13:5,9, we will mention here some talk that isn't obviously vile, demanding, or bragging - but subtle. Yet the words **do not flow from a heart of love**.

A lot that **flows out** through our mouth is *GOSSIP*. We believers, born of the Spirit, often don't think we gossip, because it is so much a part of our ordinary conversations. And without realizing it, we reap the consequences of what we speak. A person who gossips said, "But I need to talk to someone and share my pain that is related to others in my family. I'll go crazy if I don't. And I am interested in knowing about the pain and faults of others, because I, and those I share their difficulties with, can pray for them. And furthermore, I don't trust anyone who isn't open and doesn't tell all the negative facts about themselves."

> When we hear and pass along knowledge of others' sins or unfortunate situations so we can pray for them, it can be good and well intentioned, can't it? Maybe. Maybe not. For example, accountability partners / groups are intended for good, but usually end up being legalistic with the goal of keeping a person "toeing the mark" or obeying religious principles, rather than encouraging a change of heart to truth.

> As a counselor, I frequently hear men and women tell me that they had an accountability partner for a long time, but nothing much had changed. Accountability relationships often thrive on hearing about a spouse's, or another's, wrong doing *(gossip)* and on repeated confession of sin rather than pointing to the cross and truth.

> Have you ever noticed that usually when a person begins spreading "news", or gossip, or being critical, that their speech can become enlivened, and animated, and louder? When unloving speech is a *consistent behavior pattern,* it identifies the heart of that person.

There is a person whose conversations over the years constantly includes these questions / statements:

"Did you know?"
"Have you heard?"
"Did you hear?"
"I am the last to know anything!"

This person wants to be the first to know and the first to tell. These individuals have to be "in the know". They have itching ears and desire "tasty morsels". I recall one woman saying that when she grew up, the most fun she had was not playing with the other kids but sitting on the front porch and listening to the adults as they gathered and talked about the short-comings and difficulties of family and acquaintances. This was what they did for entertainment. **She said it was like dessert or food to her.**

She hadn't heard the scripture, "The words of a whisperer are like **dainty morsels**, And they go down into the innermost parts of the body." Prov. 18:8   Just listening to gossip makes us accomplices. If anyone consistently comes to us with gossip, we should not listen. As gently and tactfully as possible, we might tell the person that since the subject matter doesn't involve us, it would be best not to discuss it and be as firm as necessary.

If a friend of yours heavily criticizes a certain other and puts them down because of this or that, and then later you hear the same friend tell the other person how great they are, you see their hypocrisy. But just know if your friend continually criticizes or gossips **to you about others**, he/she will criticize or gossip **about you to others** as well. We are told that **we should not closely associate with a gossip!**

A certain person who said, "It isn't gossip if it is true", didn't know that if it is negative / hurtful, it is not to be passed on! In short, *gossip* is any communication that can be damaging to others. **Even if the tales we spread pass the test of facts, *they still must pass the test of love.*** "He who covers a transgression seeks love, but he who repeats a matter separates the best of friends" Prov. 17:9. To love is to cover an offense Prov 10:12; I Peter 4:8 and not tell others about it.

We are to **avoid worldly and empty chatter,** for it will lead to further ungodliness. James 1:26 Scripture tells us to "Let no unwholesome word proceed from your mouth, but only such a word as is good for edification *(building up and enlightening others in Christ)* according to the need of the moment, so that it will give grace to those who hear." Eph. 4: 29 We are to help strengthen and stabilize others in the body of Christ. A talebearer reveals secrets, but trustworthy people conceal those negative or hurtful things. Prov. 11:13

Sometimes we all are guilty of unloving conversation, but we are to be growing beyond that. Of course it is OUT of THE HEART that WE SPEAK, and *if we aren't walking in love*, then "the tongue is a fire, the very world of iniquity; the tongue is set among our members as that which defiles the entire body, and sets on fire the course of our life. James 3:6-8 To **guard our mouth** is to *guard against our own ruin*. Eph. 4:29 Gossip slanders others. It can destroy a person's character or personal reputation.

Other types of negative speaking also flow out of our mouth. It may be *innuendo* of some kind. And being *critical is negative,* whether it is direct or indirect. And yes, we all have been guilty of it. It can be more subtle than gossip, and it may or may not hurt others. When negativity is my lifestyle, I am not growing and living in my freedom in Christ.

Impatience is usually expressed through our words. It is **negative**, and when it is fairly constant in the life of a believer, it isn't from a heart of obedience that is maturing in love and bearing the fruit of the spirit.

Speculating and assuming about others' motives, actions or words **is negative**. And it is a HUGE thing that goes on! Some people ALWAYS assume other's intents in what they do or say. And they are so often wrong. Even if they are right, they are NOT to do it. People who speculate are drawn to focus on the negative and then they verbally spread their assumptions with others. It *reveals the condition of their heart/soul* when they consistently say something like, "He thinks he is so important doing so and so." Or, "I know they did (or think) so and so, because such and such happened..." or "I know he said this or that, but what he meant was thus and so."

We are told to **cast down speculations** and **take those thoughts captive to Christ's obedience**, (His mind-set), because the thoughts exalt themselves against our knowing God. II Cor. 10:5 We are to refuse foolish and ignorant **speculations**, knowing that they produce quarrels. II Tim. 2:23 One of the most damaging beliefs that one can verbalize is, "If he/she doesn't deny such and such when asked, then it is true." It is so wrong to make that assumption!

Grumbling and **fault-finding** characterizes Mr. S.'s speech. He is known to remark that he is just being realistic and merely states the facts. He adds, "This is a defiled world we live in, and I don't live in pretense." But remember, everything that is a fact is not TRUTH. 1 Cor. 10:23 tells us that "All things are lawful, but not all things are **profitable.** All things are lawful, but not all things **edify."**

We should let our speech be **clear (simple, direct, open)**, not indirect or with insinuations. A lot of people are raised where the family has been programmed to "talk in code" and insinuate. It is normal to them. They *assume* everyone insinuates and try to interpret others' meanings. They do not like people who are "direct". But misunderstandings result without clear and direct communication which is to be done with wisdom, discretion, gentleness, meekness, and humility. **"So also you, unless you utter by the tongue speech that is clear,**

how will it be known what is spoken? For you will be speaking into the air." I Cor. 14:9 So let our *yes* be *yes* and our *no* be *no*. Matt. 5:37

When I was a child, I used to speak like a child, think like a child, reason like a child; when I became a man *(mature),* I did away with childish things. 1 Cor. 13:11 Be sound in speech which is **beyond** reproach, so that the opponent will be put to shame, having nothing bad to say about you. Titus 2:8)

> "The one who **desires LIFE, to LOVE** and **see good days,** must **keep his tongue** from evil and his lips from speaking deceit. 1 Peter 3:10 "…**Speaking** the **truth** *in love*, we are to **grow up** *in all aspects into Him who is the head, even Christ*. Eph. 4:15. This is when we are being conformed to Godliness. We are to let EVERYTHING we do be done in LOVE. 1 Cor. 16:14

If anyone advocates a different doctrine and **does not agree with** sound words, those of our Lord Jesus Christ, and with **the doctrine** *conforming to godliness*, he is conceited *and* understands nothing; but he has a morbid interest in *controversial questions and disputes about words*, out of which arise envy, strife, abusive language, evil suspicions. 1 Tim. 6:3-4

Remind *them* of these things, and solemnly charge *them* in the presence of God **not to wrangle about words, which is useless and leads to the ruin of the hearers.** Be DILIGENT to PRESENT YOURSELF (as already) APPROVED to GOD as a *workman* who does not need to be ashamed, accurately handling the word of truth. But avoid worldly and empty chatter, for it will lead to further ungodliness, and their talk will *spread like gangrene*. 2 Tim. 2:12-17

That is LOVE in The Present Tense

CHAPTER 20

Respectful to *Them*? They Don't Deserve Respect

To LOVE another is one BEING

respectful. It has nothing to do with whether the other person *deserves* respect or not. **It is our BEING who we are in Christ.** It is to prefer others or give deference to another (over ourselves) by being attentive, patient, listening, treating them with kindness even if we don't agree with them. Yes, this may go against our feelings. But *feelings can't be trusted*. We aren't to walk by feelings - but according to the Spirit and Truth. After we begin the walk of growing up in Christ, it takes time and is a process for emotions to begin to line up.

I have heard it said that we are being fake if we don't act according to our emotions/feelings. Not so! Damaging and fearful emotions are a result of our wrong thinking…our fleshly mind-set or attitude. So we are to purpose that our human mind-set be transformed to the attitude / mind-set of Christ (Rom.12:2; Phil.2:5-8) which dwells in our spirit.

That MIND-SET is LOVE - which is *humility*, the attitude of *a servant*, not regarding one's self, but *giving ourselves up* for others as He gave Himself up for us. Eph.5:2 Remember that Jesus was persecuted and suffered as He gave Himself up – sacrificed Himself - for us. This is the image and likeness of Christ. And today, whoever would be Godly – meaning whoever would desire to be conformed to Godliness - to His attitude and the resulting actions - will to some degree be persecuted maybe by false accusations, insults, etc. 2 Tim.3:12 And this is when we suffer for His sake. Phil.1:29 Often, any adversity can be the prod we need to BRING us to submission and allowing His attitude to pre-vail in us during hard times.

The term, **"for His sake"** means for the *purpose of being conformed to His mind-set and image so that others would see Him through us* and desire to also become disciples John.13:34 - and that we would experience Him - *know Him* - more intimately as we walk in daily life. **Eternal LIFE** is our **knowing God** and His LIFE. When we LOVE others, it is to LOVE God and to *KNOW HIM in the fellowship of His sufferings* and in *the power of His resurrection*. Phil.3:10

"This is **life eternal**, that they might **know you** the only true **God**, and Jesus Christ, whom you have sent. John 17:3 This is our calling and His very purpose for those who are new creations with His life in them, those who are His possession.

When someone falsely accuses us

Or does something evil against us, it is hard. My sweet friend said of this kind of love., "But that is SO HARD to do!" *Yes, it can be beyond hard IF we aren't "preppers"!* If *our minds aren't prepared and gird-ed with truth - in advance*. 1 Peter 1:13-14 If we wait until we are blind-sided and our emotions are taking over, it IS hard. At the same time, I repeat, growing in this is a process. But the choice to Love in this way is not as hard if we remember we *have been equipped* by Christ's LIFE and POWER in us to do this.

It can be difficult even when we ARE prepared and are hit by loss, unfairness, false accusations, etc., out of nowhere. Christ Himself suffered rejection and shaming. Often it is hard to keep our focus on the Truth and trust Christ as our Life, Provision, Protection and the Power in us that enables us to respond with love - esteeming others better than ourselves. It was even **hard on Jesus** when He asked the Father, " IF it be your will, take this cup from me.." But as He said, we are to love our enemies and pray for those who persecute us. Matt. 5:44 It's easy to love those that love us, do things for us, appreciate us, and think as we think.

When we are hit by unfairness - especially if it is often by the same person(s), we usually want to tell others so they can pray for us. But our sharing it *can* turn into gossip. We can become critical. A person once told me that if something is true, it isn't gossip or being critical! WRONG! *Sometimes those people do outer works that give the APPEARANCE of true service, giving, and putting others above themselves. But their mouths speak the intent of the heart.*

> We are instructed to love these people, yet we can love them without having to be in close fellowship with them. We aren't to speculate about them. We are to do nothing from selfishness or empty conceit, but with humility of mind regard one another as more important than ourselves. Phil.2:3 We are exhorted to walk in love, just as Christ also loved us and GAVE HIMSELF UP for us, an offering and A SACRIFICE to God as a fragrant aroma. Eph.5:2

God's PURPOSE and plan for us is for His grace, love and His likeness to be seen and experienced through us. John.13:34 For us to bear His fruit - the FRUIT OF THE SPIRIT which is love, joy, peace, patience, kindness, goodness, faithfulness, gentleness, self-control; against such things there is no law. Gal.5:22-23

"A new commandment I give to you, that you love one another, even as I have loved you, that you also love one another. *By this* all men will *know that you are My disciples*, if you have love for one another." John.13:34-35 Love is the proof to others of our being believers who belong to Christ.

When the word of God says that **perfect love casts out fear,** it means that in one who is maturing (being perfected) in loving others, fear is being cast away from the one who loves. There is no fear in love; but perfect love casts out fear, because fear involves torment and the **one who fears is not perfected in love.** We love, *because* He first loved us. *If someone says, "I love God," and hates his brother, he is a liar; for the one who does not love his brother whom he has seen, cannot love God whom he has not seen.* 1 John 4:20

That is LOVE in the Present Tense

CHAPTER 21

Angry? Offended? Giving Others Control Over Us?

They *Make* Me Feel

A few weeks ago, a guy interviewed on television said that he had **a right to be offended** and that **whenever one is offended, it is always another's fault** because they say or do offensive things. He said that anytime anyone does or says offensive things, they should be made to be silent. And that one should protest in such a case. He didn't realize that his protest might hurt or offend others! He didn't understand that one person might be offended by a specific circumstance while another would not. It is all interpreted from one's own human mindset - one's heart.

Remember, it is out of the heart that our mouth speaks. Luke 6:45 I just heard a woman on a news broadcast say, **"I can't feel good about myself unless circumstances and others' opinions change."** She is basing *who she is* and *how she feels* on situations and *other people*.

Another person who said he had "known his identity in Christ" for many years, told me that he had recently experienced some other people being **condescending** and **speaking down to him.** He added that **he has a hard time trusting the intentions of anyone** who acts like that toward him for any reason... someone degrading him. He was offended... and angry.

He was still putting his trust in people – which scripture never tells us to do. And *he was speculating about their intentions*. After some long talks and some hard times of LEARNING to respond to others out of his identity in Christ, he realized that he had not truly been appropriating Christ's indwelling life and power. Nowhere are we to trust in another's words or actions to feel of worth, secure, and live with joy and peace.

So our anger begins in US - NOT because of others. It begins in our heart, our mind, our thinking...our wrong thinking. We reason *according to the wisdom of the world system* that tells us people, status, places, things should fulfill us and are responsible for how we think and feel about ourselves and that things must be fair. We can live with anger and disappointment if we continue to think that others MAKE US FEEL - are responsible for - how we see ourselves and for our emotions!

> We might call it frustration. Or disgust. Or impatience. Or irritation. Or being offended. Sometimes we deny it. We blame others - or our circumstances. We believe we have a right to be angry. Or offended. Or impatient. Anger can come from our feeling hurt or ignored. We can feel as if we are victims.

> **What causes anger? Where does it originate?** Most of us would say it comes from what others do or do not do. But why? Most would admit it is because we believe we are blocked from having something that is our right to have. Or that it is from grief or hurt. So we get angry and ATTEMPT to CONTROL others and our circumstances to get what we want and/or find healing from hurt. And it doesn't work, so we fight, blame and demand.

But WHY would we feel THE NEED TO BE IN CONTROL? We often try to "fix" others and circumstances *to make things turn out right* for us. We can compete to be right, to be the best, so we will be recognized and get what we feel we deserve. We attempt to control so we will feel *Secure. Significant. Accepted. Content. Not lonely.* Trying to be in control is an endeavor to meet these inner needs. **But THIS is what it means to walk according to the flesh - old false beliefs and the resulting FEELINGS and behaviors.**

Sometimes we try to control by holding it in, by withholding. Sometimes we try to control others by venting verbally or physically. Sometimes we are angry at ourselves and hurt ourselves because we feel we are losers. But whatever way we express our anger, it leads to confusion, pain, deception, methods of escape, fights, quarrels, disputes, immorality, even riots, and so on.. And our ways of trying to control life backfire on us.

> When we believe we must be in control, we can interpret even good intentions as put-downs. We carry anger, offenses, and become critical and act in ways to change others, or take revenge on those whom we believe offended us. When we do this, we GIVE CONTROL of OURSELVES over TO THEM! By this, it shows that we aren't taking responsibility *over our own mind, thinking, beliefs*.

Someone told me that when he is in a worship service the **music itself makes him feel** joyful, and he didn't ever want to lose that feeling. EMOTIONS to *that* person REPRESENT TRUTH. The person relies on emotions to guide him in what he does. He relies on his feelings and believes they can be trusted.

Many of us think that if we don't EXPRESS what we FEEL, we are being FAKE – not real. They need to know that frustrating and damaging emotions/feelings DO NOT represent Truth. Well we can't **count on** FEEINGS to represent Truth.

Recently, I was talking with a believer who has been in church all of his life and has read the Bible or Christian literature almost every day for years. He had always tried to do what was right and lead a moral life. He is retired and was telling me how he was just now realizing how he had walked by FEELINGS all of his life. And without considering what he was doing, he had made decisions and responded to people and circumstances out of the way he **felt**. He was letting his **perception** of others' responses and attitudes **control him**.

His inclination was to speculate ad interpret others' actions as rejection and had learned to withdraw and put up walls to avoid getting hurt. He had believed feelings represented truth. And he would suppress his anger. But now he is learning Truth and has learned that **it often FEELS RISKY to walk in the Truth.** He is learning to respond with the attitude of Christ and in doing so, his walls are crumbling down. He says he already has more joy and peace than in all of the previous years of his life!

We think we need to be *compatible* with another who has the same beliefs and likes in order to love them. Of course while thinking that, we must know to LOVE is to prefer the other above one's self, to humble one's self and serve, letting go of one's own human / fleshly desires. We *will* suffer rejections and put-downs and even others lying about us. *But **another mystery** is that God will use these very times to work His will and way in us.*

There is a way for our thinking and our emotions to be changed. And the only way is that we would know truth and our thinking would be brought in line with the attitude of Christ. When this mind-set is our focus and we continue in it as we forgive others, our hurt and anger that is so destructive to us, will be healed. How many people know this? **It is one of the mysteries of God Himself**.

But worldly wisdom – our own reason that makes human sense to us - is A PARADOX - the very OPPOSITE of the wisdom and truth that comes from God. And PRIDE is involved in the wisdom of the world. Who is wise and understanding **among us? Let us show it by a good life, by deeds done in the humility** that comes **from Godly wisdom**. We are not to harbor bitter envy and selfish ambition in our hearts, or boast or deny the truth.

Such "wisdom" does not come down from heaven but is earthly, un-spiritual, demonic. For where we have ENVY and SELFISH AMBITION, there we find DISORDER and every EVIL PRACTICE. But the wisdom that comes from heaven is first of all *pure*; then *peace-loving, con-siderate, submissive, full of mercy and good fruit, impartial and sin-cere*. Peacemakers who sow in peace reap a harvest of righteousness. James 3: 13-18

> What causes *fights* and *quarrels* among us? Don't they come from *our desires that battle within us*? We desire but do not have, so we kill. We covet but cannot get what we want, so we quarrel and fight. We do not have because we do not ask God. When we ask and do not receive, it is because we ask with wrong motives, that we may spend what we get on our pleasures (which includes status and being recognized). James 4:1-3

So what IS God's way – His wisdom? It is opposite of pride – the WAY of the world system. His WAY is for believers who have received His unconditional love and forgiveness, have been born of His Spirit be-coming new creations in Him, who know their needs are met in Him, and who know they have been equipped and made adequate to live out His way. And God's way is the WAY of LOVE and HUMILITY where the focus is not on us and on getting what we think we deserve or what we think will fulfill us or make us secure.

The heavenly or higher way is expressed by the attitude and mind of

Christ, and it is to be OUR FOCUS. Although Jesus' IDENTITY is God, **He didn't regard His being God a thing to cling to or be used for His own advantage**. Instead, He emptied Himself to take on the form of a bond-servant, being made in the likeness of men. And He humbled Himself by becoming obedient to the point of death, even death on a cross. Phil. 2:5-8

Jesus, knowing that under the New Covenant to come, people who were born of His Spirit would be endued with the power to receive and respond, said, "But to you who are listening I say: Love your enemies, do good to those who hate you, bless those who curse you, pray for those who mistreat you. If someone slaps you on one cheek, turn to them the other also. If someone takes your coat, do not withhold your shirt from them. Give to everyone who asks you, and if anyone takes what belongs to you, do not demand it back. Do to others as you would have them do to you."

"If you love those who love you, what credit is that to you? Even sinners love those who love them. And if you do good to those who are good to you, what credit is that to you? Even sinners do that. And if you lend to those from whom you expect repayment, what credit is that to you? Even sinners lend to sinners, expecting to be repaid in full. But love your enemies, do good to them, and lend to them without expecting to get anything back. Luke 6: 27-35

This takes humility with one trusting Christ in him. This **lowliness of heart** is an **enigma to our natural** and **fleshly ways of thinking**. God's way is impossible to understand with human reason. *It is hard to fathom that humility triumphs over a show of strength and having to win and having to be recognized. But it is where real power comes from!* Love and serving - putting others first – before ourselves – is how Christ reigns and how believers can reign in life.

Love doesn't take into account wrongs done to one. To LOVE others

152

is giving and serving – not getting. Love is patient, love is kind and is not jealous; love does not brag and is not arrogant, It perseveres and hopes. And as a result of walking in love, we partake of what is ALREADY ours in Christ - the inner reward of true joy, peace and a clear conscience. 1 Cor. 13, Heb. 9:14, 10:22

Let us be reminded again that changing our mind to grow up and persevere in love and humility is a process and it takes time.

But it is **worth it** to KNOW GOD in this way. When we *know God*.. we don't get "more of the Holy Spirit" or get "closer to Him". We *EXPERIENCE more intimacy* with Him Who is already our Life, Protection and Sufficiency

That is LOVE in the Present Tense

CHAPTER 22

Questions & Answers re: Love & Humility

- **Does serving others mean we do everything that is asked or demanded of us?**

No. We must use wisdom to choose what we should or should not do. Serving is a voluntary choice. We are not to over-commit out of fear of rejection. We are not to reward selfish, emotionally dependent, or abusive people *so they will accept us*. That enables them to continue in their ways. It takes practice and discernment, while relying on God's strength, to learn how to respond and give an humble answer to people who use insults and threaten with words to get what they want.

We are NOT to receive their critical words as truth about ourselves, *because we know who we are as new creations in Christ and His sufficiency in us*. But we are to put on a heart of compassion, kindness, humility, gentleness, patience, and be forgiving just as the Lord forgave us. Col. 3:12-13

- **Should we associate with those who say they are believers but are consistently threatening / insulting?**

We must be warned to not engage in cycles of debates about words, or with threatening, accusing, and verbally abusive people. It may not be wise to be *best* friends with these people. We need to learn to draw boundaries for ourselves regarding people who may betray us. This doesn't mean we shouldn't associate with them. But we must be loving if or when we do.

We are to be courageous in trusting Christ and not in ourselves, and not be threatened by others' threats! A wise person will listen to others without arguing and drop his/her end of the rope. The wise can back off even if he is "right". He can wisely and gently repeat back what he heard the other say to show he is listening. This can be disarming to the other person. It is only by Christ's power in us that we can do this. We can do this even *as we learn to draw appropriate boundaries and state* **our limitations – not theirs.**

We can confront them without doing harm. *We are to return criticism, insults, or unfairness with humility and soft answers that emerge from a heart of love.* Gentle answers turn away wrath. (Prov. 15:1) If we answer foolish people in the same way they talk to, or reason with us, we make ourselves like them (foolish)! (Prov. 26:4) At the same time, we have to be firm in establishing borders *for ourselves* with abusive people.

What about people who look as if they are serving others but who are critical, negative and gossipy?

Efforts to find appreciation by serving others may look good and humble to an observer, but if that person does not have peace and joy and is not fulfilled, it is because the service hasn't been from a heart of a servant, but rather from efforts to find approval and fulfillment from others. Typically this is an angry and critical person who often tries to conceal the anger and who gossips. Scripture tells us not to associate with a person who gossips. Prov. 20:19

The woman who once said to me. "If it is true, it isn't gossip!" NOT SO. She needed to know if it is negative, damaging communication about another, *it is gossip.* The same woman emphasized, "I might be critical, but I am certainly NOT negative." OK. I was thinking to myself that if being critical **isn't negative,** what IS it?

- **What about my *feelings*? My feelings were hurt. I have a right to get respect. Shouldn't there be more laws against those who do and say offensive things? I was offended.**

"They offended me - hurt my *feelings*" is huge in today's society. Individuals are often raised in an environment where people subtly get the message that they are victims, and they hold others responsible for their well-being. They feel entitled. They tend to interpret words as put-downs whether that was the intent or not, especially if they are *insecure* about their worth. They seek to find worth and security in opinions of others. **A reminder - when we hold others responsible for how we *feel*, then we GIVE control of ourselves to others!** We must not operate on a feeling level.

Issues *of the heart cannot be legislated.* (No one has a *right* to get respect.) We must take responsibility for our own feelings. When we trust the Lord and embrace our identity in Christ, no one else can damage our emotions. *Our hurt feelings that are destructive result from our own perceptions and beliefs.* We need to change our mind-set - our heart - in order for our emotions to change. And it may take time. But it is *our* choice, because others cannot control our feelings. It is not what the other person *says* that offends me even if they intend to offend! It is what *I think* about what the other says. So **I am responsible** if I am offended!

We all have been hurt by lies and misunderstanding, and healing growth takes time. We can *choose to have our feelings hurt* by something others do, but their words do not have power over us. Jesus told his followers, "Blessed are **you** when men **hate you**, and ostracize **you**, and insult **you**, and scorn **your** name as evil, for the sake of the Son of Man. *(for the sake of* means *for the purpose of)* maturing in His likeness - *in love.* This is when we walk in love that others see Christ in us and come to know us as His disciples. John 13:35 So leap for joy for great is your reward. Luke 6:22

- **How do I respond to people who are unfair or try to take advantage of me? My tendency is to be indignant, angry and lash out.**

We may have to get out of our comfort zone in learning to humble ourselves and serve. We can be in the process of renewing our minds / hearts, but our old programmed emotions may surface, and it may feel scary or uncomfortable to respond with a new attitude of gentleness and patience. But we must walk through the feelings while holding onto truth if we are to grow. And it takes time.

A church member was indignant. He was telling various others, "There is one thing for sure. I WILL NOT be taken advantage of by anybody! That person who has tried to impose on me needs to be put in his place, and I am going to expose him for what he is and tell him what a jerk he is!" The church member was on-guard, likely because he had been unfairly treated in the past. **He needs to be wise and discerning about matters of business and set limitations about what he will accept,** but know that humility of heart and a gentle response are of greater benefit than slander and revenge.

- **Is it possible to compete in sports, in academics, or business and still be humble, without pride?**

Yes. It is possible, but how often does it happen with myself and others? Pride comes with looking to get accolades or win in order to establish a sense of worth or security for myself. If that is my focus and I depend on my efforts – on my winning or being exalted in some way to find what only God provides - it results in my empti-ness and pride.

- **How do we live where there are put-downs, rejections and false accusations from angry people in our home or on our jobs?**

Humility does not mean we do not speak up, be assertive and explain things if we are being abused or lied about. We should speak up *un-less* it is to protect our own fleshly way. ***Humility doesn't mean we should not draw appropriate boundaries or limitations for ourselves.*** We should. (***We can't draw boundaries for others***.) With Godly wisdom, decide what is appropriate to say and do without being de-fensive, argumentative, haughty or demanding.

Respond **firmly** with all humility and gentleness, with patience, showing tolerance for **one another** in **love.** Eph. 4:2 "But love your enemies, and do good, and lend, expecting nothing in return; and your **reward** will be **great**, and you will be sons of the Most High; for He Himself is kind to ungrateful and evil men." Luke 6:35

It may be that we need to separate ourselves from ongoing physical abuse. Proverbs 22:24 tells us to not associate with a person *given* **to anger** – meaning it is a *continual characteristic* of that person. Do not be intimidated by threats. We may need to go to another in the body of Christ to get help and advice, being careful not to gossip and spread slanderous facts about that angry person. We *are* to stand against evil - with humility.

> All who desire to live **Godly** in Christ Jesus **will be persecuted** for the sake of Christ. *For His sake* means we experience trials and put-downs, or even being misunderstood, for the purpose of our maturing in Christ and *knowing him and others seeing who Christ is through us*. II Tim. 3:12 The result will be our knowing and experiencing victory.

To sum it up, all of you be harmonious, sympathetic, broth-erly, kindhearted, and humble in spirit; not returning evil for evil or insult for insult, but giving a blessing instead; for you were called **for the very purpose that you might inherit a blessing**. Who is there to harm you if you prove zealous for what is good? But even if you should suffer for the sake of righteousness, you are blessed. And do not fear their intimida-tion, and do not be troubled. 1 Peter 3: 8-14

- **How do I disagree and yet be humble?**

Most of us have had conversations with a close friend or spouse with whom we disagree. In it all, *putting on the attitude of Christ always takes practice. But in doing so, our mind / heart will grow in being conformed to His image and likeness.* Believe me, I am acquainted with the pride of not wanting to look wrong or be misunderstood. But if I will humble myself, abide in Christ's power in me, knowing that He is my identity and defense, I can just drop my needing to prove my point. Those of us who feel a need to trump what others say, are to exercise that same obedience of faith. Do you know anyone who would rather win – or rather be right - than to have peace?

We have to remember that this kind of growth is a lifetime process. It is not learned overnight nor by merely reading these words.

That is LOVE in the Present Tense

CHAPTER 23

The Works of Law vs The Obedience of Faith

Our Nation has faced some Hard Times

Recently, there are many who are very uneasy and much concerned that the Media, the Schools, and the Government may be trying to mandate or legislate the thoughts, intents and beliefs of the people. It can be subtle. But we saw earlier in these writings that **the desires and intents of the heart** cannot be controlled by law - even God's Law. Our mind / heart can be deceived, but these things **cannot be legislated.**

I had a couple of people tell me

that words and exhortations to believers to CHOOSE to live out LOVE toward others can **"sound like *religious legalism"***. A few examples are that they think to *persevere*, to *fight the fight* of FAITH, to *run the race* of FAITH, and to *discipline ourselves* for the purpose of Godliness, is being a religious legalist. A *"legalist"* believes that one *must do certain outer works to find acceptance with God*. Based on their comments, and wanting to clarify, I will mention a bit about the difference in **Works of Law** vs the **Obedience of faith.**

Faith means to have trust, confidence and full assurance that everything the Word says about who Christ is IN and FOR us is true. Believers must by FAITH *choose for LOVE to be expressed*, because exercising FAITH is **not only** believing God's LOVE *FOR* me, what He has UNCONDITIONALLY *GIVEN* me, that He will *NEVER LEAVE* me, and that He is my *SUFFICIENCY* and *PROTECTION* and *LIFE*.

It is **BECAUSE** of those things that we are exhorted to walk in the OBEDIENCE of FAITH which includes **inner** choices and perseverance. And this OBEDIENCE is **Faith expressing itself through LOVE**. Gal. 5:6   And it is all that matters.

On the other hand, the **Works of Law** are called "religious legalism" and among other things, it is trying to keep the 10 Commandments (the Old Covenant Law and other religious rules) by doing outer works that are **not empowered** *by the Spirit – the attitude of Christ within a person.*

LOVING others is one's **OBEDIENCE** of **FAITH**. Rom.1:5; 16:26 and is an entirely different thing than one's obedience of WORKS of religious LAW. In religion, it has been supposed that people are to obey rules and Commandments to EARN acceptance from God - which would be one trying to do good works, but then always failing to live up to the law's commands.

On the other hand, a believer is ALREADY unconditionally loved and accepted forever by God, and has been born again and joined with Christ's spirit which **equips the believer** to walk in the INNER OBEDIENCE of exercising FAITH. This obedience of faith is our **GROWING** up in **HUMILITY** and **LOVE**. It is our **SOUL** being PERFECTED in LOVE. 1 John 2:5, 4:12,17,18; 1 Peter 1:22

We must remember that since learning to walk in faith and LOVE is a maturing process, we will sometimes "miss the mark" and FALL DOWN and skin our knees on the way. But that is okay. We *choose not to condemn ourselves* because God doesn't condemn us. (We must know that our being *convicted* of sin is NOT condemnation!) And we get back up and continue to **walk with our eyes and mind focused on Truth** - on same mind-set as Christ Phil. 2:5-8, which is to PUT ON the ATTITUDE (mind-set) of HUMILITY, LOVE and SERVICE to others, PREFERRING them ABOVE OURSELVES. Rom.12:10 and GIVING OURSELVES UP for them as Christ gave Himself up for the church. Eph. 5:2

This is when we PUT ON the Lord Jesus Christ, and make no provision for the flesh in regard to *its* lusts. Rom. 13:14 When our FOCUS is living from, and *clothing ourselves* with, that attitude of Christ, the fleshly beliefs and behaviors are left behind.

In choosing this, we are being transformed.

We are not to be conformed to this world, but BE TRANSFORMED by the renewing of our mind, SO THAT we may PROVE what THE WILL of GOD is, that which is good and acceptable and perfect. Rom. 12:2 When a believer is encouraged to do good works, *they are the WORKS of FAITH which flow out as a result of the renewing of the mind.*

These works of FAITH are the fruit of the spirit being expressed by LOVE. This being TRANSFORMED is when we have, in obedience to the truth, PURIFIED our SOULS for a sincere LOVE of the brethren, and fervently love one another from the heart, because we ALREADY have *been born again* not of seed which is perishable but imperishable, *that is*, through the living and enduring word of God. 1 Peter 1:22-23

For we are His workmanship, CREATED in Christ Jesus *FOR* GOOD

WORKS, which God prepared beforehand so that we would walk in them. Eph. 2:8-9 These GOOD WORKS of FAITH are NOT done to find favor with God nor to get something from God, nor to try to "pay God back" for His free gifts to us, because He has ALREADY given believers all spiritual things that relate to true life and Godliness. 2 Peter 1:3 For it is by grace you have been saved, through faith—and this is not from yourselves, it is the gift of God - not by works, so that no one can boast. Eph. 2:8-9 NIV

It is **because** of this that believers are told to DO GOOD, to be RICH in GOOD WORKS, to be generous and ready to share, storing up for themselves the treasure of a good foundation for their future, SO THAT they may TAKE HOLD OF (enjoy) that which is LIFE indeed. 1 Tim. 6:18-19 That is referring to God's LIFE which ALREADY indwells us as new creations.

When we *walk in a manner consistent with who we ALREADY ARE in Him*, we more fully EXPERIENCE those inner things. And we ACCESS by faith that grace in which we (already) stand! Rom. 5:2 That is what Paul meant when he said, "Not that I have already obtained it or have already become perfect (in soul and body), but I PRESS ON so that I may LAY HOLD OF that for which also I was (*already*) laid hold of by Christ Jesus." Phil 3:12

> To this end also we pray for you always, that our God will count you worthy of your calling, and fulfill every DESIRE for GOODNESS and the WORK of FAITH with power, (and the reason is) SO THAT the name of our Lord Jesus will be GLORIFIED IN YOU, and YOU IN HIM, according to the grace of our God and the Lord Jesus Christ. 2 Thess. 1: 11-12 This is when others see Jesus in us. It is His PURPOSE for us.

Jesus revealed that the whole religious law is fulfilled in one word

- LOVE - which is fruit of Christ's spirit and attitude within us. Because of this, the PURPOSE of a believer's walk in this life is to walk in the OBEDIENCE of FAITH to change his/her thinking to conform with Christ's mind-set of LOVE - and live it out so others can see and experience Him through us. Believers are called to the OBEDIENCE that comes from FAITH for His name's sake. Rom 1:5

> All of this repetitive, but must remember that our OBEDIENCE of FAITH is not only believing what God has done and will do FOR US. It is *exercising faith* to **LOVE others**. This is an INNER CHOICE to humble one's self, GIVE ONE'S SELF UP - just as Christ gave himself up - for others. ***It is in that same manner that God's Spirit in us is to be expressed outwardly.***

> Love is to have the attitude of a servant. It is to prefer others above one's self. It is to inwardly become of no reputation *- **not using one's identity in Christ to one's own advantage.*** Phil. 2:5-8, Gal. 2:20, Eph. 5:2

Having the attitude of a servant is NOT just an outward physical service nor giving the appearance of wisdom, religion, and self-abasement – which is of the flesh. It's not in taking pride in one's outer performance or religious appearance, which is not from the heart. It is to set our human MIND on the Spirit – on **following His example of having a mind-set of faith and LOVE**, and any outer works will appear as A RESULT.

It is not always easy to choose this way, especially in the face of hard times, and false accusation, rejection, etc. But we are urged to stand firm and endure in this – in our obedience of faith – which is to STRIVE for the FAITH - and it *doesn't* just mean striving to do good behaviors or outer works. Phil. 1:27

Our persevering with **the *attitude* of a servant is** our *discipline for*

Godliness because Godliness is profitable for all things, since it holds promise for the PRESENT LIFE and *also* for the *life* to come. This is a trustworthy statement deserving full acceptance. Because **it is for this we LABOR and STRIVE (in faith),** because we have fixed our hope on the living God, who is the Savior of all men, especially of believers.1 Tim. 4:7-10

We are to PURSUE our being conformed in our Human mind / SOUL to the righteousness, godliness, faith, love, perseverance, *and* gentleness (that ALREADY indwells our spirit). This is when we **fight the good fight of faith** and take hold of (now) the eternal life to which we were called... 1 Tim. 6:11-12a

To **fight the good fight of faith** and **to strive in faith** is our laboring to **fervently hold on to exercising by faith the mind-set of Christ** – especially through hard times - which results in the fruit of spirit and in love being expressed outwardly.

Believers were being commended by Peter when he said, "you have PURIFIED your SOULS *by obedience to the truth* for sincere mutual **LOVE**, love for one another." 1 Peter 1:22 **This is our being perfected** (maturing) **in LOVE.** And *expressing LOVE is our obedience to truth.* We sometimes hear that if we just relax and receive His love, Christ in us will automatically flow out without any choosing or effort on our part. This is a *misunderstanding* of the Word, because as we live in this world, we must choose to press on and endure in Faith for it to express itself through LOVE.

That is LOVE in the Present Tense

> To a distant observer, the outer *works of law* (works of the flesh) and the works of faith may *appear* the same. But up close, the ***obedience of faith*** is accompanied by the *fruit of the spirit* - love, joy, peace, patience, kindness, goodness,

faithfulness, gentleness and self- discipline. While the **result** of **walking after religious law / flesh** eventually leads to FEAR, shame, failure, resentment, anger, and guilty conscience.

CHAPTER 24

Be Alert – Don't Be Deceived

Today, we must be ON GUARD

as we walk by faith according to the Spirit. As we WALK in LOVE.

We must be on guard and be careful to **discern the deceivers** among us....There has been deep concern that big Technology companies and even Government has endeavored to manipulate what we see and hear. It not only arises in government, large corporations, social media and other groups, but it is even in the church. In any area, deception can arise from within - among us - or from without, to subtly draw away those who desire truth and to know God.

Deception isn't obvious. If it were, it wouldn't be deception. One might APPEAR as an ANGEL of LIGHT, even a SERVANT of RIGHTEOUSNESS. 2 Cor. 11:13-15 They advocate for the good of others – maybe even promote some Christian truths. There are a lot of truths woven into deception. It only takes a speck of non-truth to deceive. It can be leaving out part of the complete truth...not going far enough.

It can be as simple as cleverly inserting a word, or trying to prove a word has a different meaning, or leaving out a word. It may be as simple as the press or anyone saying, "They *indicated* this or that." Or "It is *regarded* by most sources that it is true…", Or, "What they did underscores *that they think* so and so…" All of this is subtle and can be APPEALING and brings what we want to hear. And we follow it. Partial truth can be quite effective for a while. Deceptions build upon other subtle deceptions. Then we wonder why we are stuck and can't get past the potholes, roadblocks, and assailants.

Since Satan is a deceiver and the FATHER of LIES, he doesn't usually show up to deceive with horns and a forked tail, but he disguises himself as an **ANGEL of LIGHT**. John 8:44 Therefore it is not surprising if his servants also DISGUISE themselves as servants of righteousness, but whose end will be according to their deeds. 2 Cor. 11:13-15 For such men are slaves, *not of Christ* but of their *own appetites*; and by their **smooth and flattering** speech they **DECEIVE** the hearts of the UNSUSPECTING. Rom. 16:18

The appeal of deception is that it is **based on the PRINCIPLES of the WORLD** system. And we need to know all that is in the world, the LUST of the FLESH and the LUST of the EYES and the boastful PRIDE of LIFE, is not from the Father, but is from the WORLD. 1 John 2:16 And these things are opposite of God's way. DECEPTIONS can be rooted in the reasoning and understanding of our human mind and desires.

Principles of the world CAN SEEM right and good, even religious. So we must BE of SOBER SPIRIT, **BE ON** the **ALERT**, because OUR ADVERSARY, THE DEVIL, PROWLS around like a ROARING LION, seeking someone to DEVOUR. 1 Peter 5:8

Believers, *having been firmly rooted and now being built up in Him and established in your faith,* just as you were instructed, *and* overflowing with gratitude….see *to it **that there is no one who takes you captive through philosophy and empty deception** in accordance with *human tradition*, in accordance with the elementary principles of the world, rather than in accordance with Christ. Col. 2:7-8

Believers who know their identity in Christ can be deceived because certain ways are so acceptable by society and the world. The things of the world as the "LUST of the FLESH" are the things that are the object of our desires - things that we think will satisfy any kind of appetite. We can think the LUST of the FLESH means only sexual lust. But it can mean greed, feeling secure in having a bank account, material things, people's acceptance. It is to live life by the senses. It can be selfish with possessions and the gratification of material desires, or by other various ways of trying to find worth or significance.

And we might think the "LUST of the EYES" would be only involve sexual type lust. But how many of us, regarding our clothing or our car, are concerned about what others will think of us if we look / dress a certain way or drive certain vehicle? Or how many of us "need" to have self or things visually "right" to feel "satisfied"? Yes. It can be as simple as that...or NOT.

The "PRIDE of LIFE" can be as simple as being prideful if we accomplish certain things to be held in high esteem, or it can be our convincing others we are "right". **When you identified your "False Beliefs", how many had to do with these prideful *things of this world*?**

> Believers who are **new creations in Christ** are told to SEE TO IT that NO ONE TAKES YOU CAPTIVE through philosophy and empty deception, according to the TRADITION of MEN, according to the elementary PRINCIPLES of the WORLD, rather than according to Christ. You can do this because in Him you **have been equipped** and made COMPLETE in Spirit, and He is the head-over all rule and authority. Col. 2: 8-10
> Be diligent to keep in mind that those who are joined with the

Lord and one spirit with Him, 1 Cor. 6:17 have been given POWER over all the powers of the enemy.

The immature in Christ can be deceived **even if they know their identity in Him**, and **believers are warned to be alert to it**. Even though deceptions NO LONGER have any POWER over us to enslave us, sin and Satan are so appealing and deceiving that it is possible to obey the desires by which we are tempted. Remember he **is the *deceiver* of the brothers and sisters in Christ.**

Paul told the **believers** at Corinth, But I am afraid that just as Eve was deceived by the serpent's cunning, **your minds** may somehow be **led astray from your sincere and pure devotion to Christ.** 2 Cor. 11:3

But each one is tempted when he is carried away and enticed by *his own* lust. Then when lust has conceived, it *gives birth to sin*; and sin, when it has run its course, brings forth death (separation from experiencing God's blessings). **Do not be deceived, my beloved *brothers and sisters*.** James 1:14-16

But prove yourselves doers of the word, and not just hearers who **deceive** *themselves.* James 1:22 Woah...We can even deceive *ourselves!* Satan is the deceiver of the whole world. Rev. 12:9 There are many deceivers out there. 1 John 1:7

In current times, a lot is being said about our needing ***unity*** in our country rather than division, but we must remember that the very people who say that can be deceivers who speak evil, accuse, lie, and slander. The word *devil* means *slanderer* or one who puts himself or something between people to ***divide*** them. Satan's goal is to divide family, society, government, church and racial relationships.... to steal, kill and destroy - ***by deception.***

Those who **are maturing in Christ** by their faith expressing itself through LOVE are **learning to discern good and evil**. For everyone who partakes only of milk is not accustomed to the word of righteousness, for he is an infant (in Christ). But solid food is for the MATURE, who because of PRACTICE, have their SENSES TRAINED to DISCERN GOOD and EVIL. Heb. 5:14

We believers who know our identity as new creations in Christ don't "automatically know" what to do. That is the reason we are told that our senses must be trained.

Believers are told to encourage one another and build up one another... TO GROW in Godliness. 1 Thess. 5:11 Today in our society, people are being deceived into thinking evil is good, and good is evil. Isaiah 5:20 says "Woe to those who call **evil good**, and **good evil**; Who *substitute darkness for light and light for darkness; Who substitute bitter for sweet and sweet for bitter!*"

We must be on alert not be tricked in this way and be overcome by **evil**, but overcome **evil** with **good**. Rom. 12:21 Love *must be* free of hypocrisy detesting what is **evil**; clinging to what is **good**. Rom.12:9

Believers are all sons of light and sons of day. We are not of night nor of darkness; so let us NOT SLEEP as others do, as again we are told, *be alert* and *sober*. 1 Thess. 5:5-7 Since we are of the day, let us be-sober and put on - and KEEP on - THE ARMOR that will protect us. We are to PUT ON the BREASTPLATE of FAITH and LOVE, and as A HELMET, the HOPE of salvation. 1 Thess. 5-8 This is our PROTECTION.

SO, to be on guard and avoid being deceived, we must be choosing to walk in the POWER that is ALREADY ours. To WALK IN the POWER we have, we must be growing, persevering, and maturing in FAITH expressing itself through LOVE.

Here again, we see the answer is to PUT ON in our human MIND what we ALREADY have in our spirit. THAT is our ARMOR.

Often, believers can be deceived by false teachings about God's grace such as "since I received Christ and am a new creation, joined with Him for eternity, and I am going to heaven when I die, what's wrong with having some immoral excitement or telling a lie as we live here and now in this world...??"

The answer is if we stumble and fall and *continue in* that way, **we experience the natural consequences of what we do – here and now**. AND we BLOCK ourselves from partaking NOW of His sufficiency, the peace, joy, and clear conscience that are ALREADY ours in Christ, and we BLOCK ourselves from walking in the overcoming power that is ours. We neglect it and wonder why!

> Therefore, knowing this beforehand, BE ON YOUR GUARD so that **you are not carried away** by the error of unprincipled men and FALL FROM your own steadfastness (of exercising faith and the resulting Godly behaviors), but GROW in the GRACE and KNOWLEDGE of our Lord and Savior Jesus Christ. To Him *be* the glory, both now and to the day of eternity. 2 Peter 3:17

Believers are urged to KEEP their EYE ON those who cause dissensions and hindrances contrary to the teaching which you learned, and TURN AWAY from them. They may even hold to a form of godliness, although they have denied its power; AVOID such men as these. Rom. 16:17-18, 2 Tim. 3:5

Since **all who desire to live godly** in Christ Jesus will be **persecuted**, we need to know that most *persecution* involves *deception*, and *accusations*. So BE AWARE that evil men and impostors will proceed from bad to worse, deceiving and being deceived. You, however,

CONTINUE in the things you have learned and become convinced of, knowing from whom (the Holy Spirit) you have learned them. 2 Tim. 3:12-14

Those who are growing in Christ, need to ...MAKE SURE no one DECEIVES them, and know that he (Satan) was a murderer from the beginning, and does not stand in the truth because there is no truth in him. Remember that whenever he speaks a lie, he speaks from his own nature, for HE IS A LIAR and the FATHER OF LIES. John 8:44 We can be tempted and deceived into thinking certain things are okay.

We are to know that, and at the same time we who are being steadfast to grow up in Christ, are to be anxious for nothing but in everything by prayer and supplication with thanksgiving let your requests be made known to God. And the PEACE of God, which surpasses all comprehension, will GUARD our HEARTS and our MINDS in Christ Jesus. Phil. 4:7

> We can be tempted and deceived into thinking certain things are okay. But we must remind ourselves that it is okay *only if it aligns with* whatever is *true*, whatever is *honorable*, whatever is *right*, whatever is *pure*, whatever is *lovely*, whatever is of *good repute*, if there is any *excellence* and if anything *worthy of praise*. We are to DWELL ON THESE things. Phil. 4:8

> We MUST by faith keep our MIND firmly SET and focused on these things and on living out the mind-set of Christ that dwells in our spirit, in order to be *transformed* by the *renewing* of our human *mind*. Remember, we do this because our MIND is the area where we can be DECEIVED. At the same time, the reasons we are being transformed and conformed to His image is so that we will **KNOW GOD** and **PROVE** to **OTHERS** what the WILL OF GOD IS, that which is good and acceptable and perfect. Phil. 4:6-8, 2:5-8, Rom. 12:2

Our purpose and **GOAL** must be to, by faith, renew our mind to these things and **GROW** to **ATTAIN** to the unity of the faith, and of the KNOWLEDGE of the SON of GOD, to a mature human, to the measure of the stature which belongs to the fullness of Christ.

As a result, we are no longer to be children, tossed here and there by waves and carried about by every wind of doctrine, by the TRICKERY of men, by craftiness in DECEITFUL scheming; Eph. 4:13-14 NIV This is our **protection** and is the way we battle the enemy. It is the very opposite of the world's way of war. At the same time, it is the way we experience more fully what is ALREADY ours in Christ.

Finally, be strong in the Lord and in the **strength** of His might. Eph. 6:10 Say to yourself, "I can do all things through Him who **strengthens** me." Phil. 4:13 I am **strengthened** with all power, according to His glorious might, for the attaining of all perseverance and patience; joyously. Col. 1:11

Speaking to the church, the Apostle Paul urged them to **not be deceived**, God is not mocked; for whatever a man sows, this he will also reap. For the one who *sows to his own flesh* will from the flesh reap corruption, but the one who sows to the Spirit will from the Spirit reap eternal life. Gal. 6:7-8

Since believers ALREADY spiritually have eternal life, if they think since their sins are forgiven and they are "going to heaven after they die", that it is okay to continuously sin, they are being deceived.

And rather than **laying hold on ETERNAL LIFE** *now in the present age* by fighting the good fight of faith, and KNOWING the only true GOD 1 Tim 6:12, John 17:3 and enjoying the Kingdom of God now - which is peace, joy and righteousness in the Holy Spirit, Rom. 14:17 *they block their experience of it and reap the natural consequences of their actions here and now.*

Recently I heard someone say the we don't grow in Grace because we already have all the Grace we need...We DO INDEED have all we need, but we are implored to **GROW** in what we ALREADY have just as the church at Philippi was told to, "be *on your guard* so that you are not carried away by the error of unscrupulous people and *lose your own firm commitment*, but **GROW IN the GRACE and KNOWLEDGE** of our Lord and Savior Jesus Christ. 2 Peter 3:18-19

The Word under the New Testament Covenant warns people NOT to be DECEIVED. It says: We are to **be on guard not to be deceived** by religious people nor by those in the world in general. If anyone thinks himself to be religious, yet does not bridle his tongue but **deceive**s his *own* heart, this person's religion is worthless. But prove yourselves doers of the word, and not just hearers who **deceive** themselves. James 1:22,26

Your adversary is like a roaring lion seeking who he may devour. And he does it by deception deceiving the minds of those who are not standing firm in faith. These *people who deceive* are grumblers and fault-finders; they follow their own evil desires; they boast about themselves and flatter others for their own advantage." Jude 1:16

That is LOVE in The Present Tense

CHAPTER **25**

Capture the Terrorists

Be Diligent. This is War.

WHAT and WHERE are the terrorists? They can lurk anywhere. Not just on the battlefield in other countries. Not just in underground webs hidden among ordinary people. Not just sprinkled among spies. And not just in our electronic devices. They can be at the root of some serious problems that are affecting our lives...some of which are very destructive. And they are where we might not suspect.

In our personal lives, we can think our circumstances and other people are the enemy – the terrorists. It feels like they are, and we have been told they are. And we wonder why the ordinary can be so hard. We are in a battle and fighting the best way we know how as we deal with daily frustrations. We war over unfairness. Fear of rejection. Loneliness. Not having enough. Incompatibility. Not being able to control situations that might be threatening our health, our life.

We don't understand the reason for our pain. We wonder why we are restless or not experiencing peace...why we feel defeated, fearful, depressed, or are in situations we can't seem to overcome. We worry. We may even pray. But nothing works. We live in a world system where our ways of thinking and our endeavors can make total sense to us and may look good or maybe even religious. Or not. But things can fall apart.

The enemy even uses our OWN pride and fleshly interactions and responses with others – our comportment – the way we present ourselves - to defeat US and cause people to turn against us and be under attack with lies and hatred.

Then someone tells us that the terrorists aren't who and what we thought they were. We are told the fact is that our enemies are not of the visible world. But the invisible. Whaaat?

Our *own* fleshly armor and strategies for life's battles haven't been adequate. But why? They could have seemed good and right. But there wasn't lasting peace, fulfillment, security…inside. We have believed we should find these things in people, performance, places and fair circumstances. And we've sought it there, and that has been our battle ground with many types of ineffective tactics. What has been behind our battle plans? What have been our weapons for our warfare? And we wonder WHAT is really the ENEMY?

Then we heard someone say their *thoughts* are their worst enemies. Even terrorists at times.

Behind our *deficient strategies* are those fleshly **deceptive BELIEFS, thoughts** and **attitudes** in our human mind that can SEEM NORMAL and ACCEPTABLE to us and to the world system. And **THAT is the reason we can be deceived**! When we walk after these beliefs, and use THEM as our ARMOR / WEAPONS, they may seem to work for a while, but eventually, we walk in personal futility and defeat. And all the while, we are being conformed to the world's system of thinking. And behind those False Beliefs are FEARS of every kind.

But as we have seen, the truth is that our struggle is not against flesh and blood, as we thought! Rather, it is against the rulers, against the authorities, against the powers of this dark world and against the spiritual forces of evil in the heavenly realms. Eph. 6:12 NIV And we try to battle with them by the world's weapons – by our human way of THINKING - by DECEPTIVE thoughts, attitudes and beliefs in our mind. But these are TERRORISTS that must be thrown down and taken CAPTIVE, because they actually DEFEAT us rather than being our adequate weapons!

The ENEMY plants these thoughts and beliefs (terrorists) in the human mind, over time. And they can remain there - even after we are born again in our spirit. These thoughts are the force behind our destructive emotions and defeating behaviors. The BATTLE is in our MIND.

We have power over the Terrorists! The Power we have is knowing the TRUTH of who Christ is in and for us and who we are in Him and our FAITH expressing itself by **LOVE**. This is our POWER over the power of the enemy! It is the OPPOSITE of the world's way of fighting. And we have been **equipped** for this war!

So believers are not to be **overcome** by evil, but **overcome** evil with good. Rom. 12:21 "Good" here means living with the inner mind-set of Christ - LOVE.

> Beliefs and attitudes are DECEPTIVE because they might SEEM okay. An example might be something as simple as, "I must please others to find acceptance". Or "I must be in control to be secure." Or "I deserve respect, and things must be fair for me to be okay." Or it might be our living by speculations about the meaning of another's words or body language.

> Maybe it is believing, "I must punish others for treating me unfairly...or just causing me inconvenience", or "The way I

feel is the fault of others or my circumstances, and my feelings represent truth." Or it can be myself not letting go of wrongs done by another because I think, "they will get away with it if I don't show them how wrong they are." But that only destroys ME and my knowing Life and Peace! These are false FLESHLY beliefs that lead to our hurtful emotions such as anger, guilt, resentment or shame....and all of the resulting behaviors.

If we aren't DILIGENT to *focus on truth* and renew our thoughts, others will control them. In addition to the old left-over fleshly beliefs that were developed in us before we were born of the spirit, the world bombards us repetitiously with thoughts that seem good, or at least, okay. And these thoughts can lead to beliefs which result in ineffective and self-defeating behaviors.

For though we walk ***in the flesh (our body with its desires), we do not war *according* to the flesh***, but I see another law at work in me, waging war against the law of my MIND and making me a prisoner of the law of sin at work within me (*my body*). So you are urged to abstain from sinful desires, which wage **war against your SOUL** (mind). What causes fights and quarrels among you? Don't they come from your **desires** that **battle within you**? 2 Cor. 10:3, Rom. 7:23, 1 Peter 2:11, James 4:1 NIV

We can think that "sinful desires" in the above scripture only means sexual lusts and desires. But these desires include the lusts of the eyes, the lusts of the flesh and the pride of life – all the things in the world that draw us.

Believers who have received God's love, grace, forgiveness and His indwelling life, are not to war with the deceptive powers of darkness according to fleshly thinking – to our human understanding - because the WEAPONS of our WARFARE are not carnal (fleshly) but mighty in God for **pulling down strongholds, casting down arguments** (and our **speculations**) and **every high thing** *that exalts itself AGAINST THE KNOWLEDGE OF GOD*, **BY bringing every THOUGHT into CAPTIVITY to the OBEDIENCE of CHRIST**. II Cor. 10:3-5

This is when we fight the good fight of faith I Tim. 6:12, and take up our cross (our trial), with the obedience (MIND-Set) of Christ, which is LOVE. Phil. 2:5-8 *Mature LOVE casts out the FEAR* that is behind our deceptive beliefs. 1 John 4:18   So LOVE is our armor.

We are to trust in the Lord with all our heart and not lean on our own understanding. There is a way that SEEMS RIGHT to humans, but its end is the way of death. Prov. 3:5;14:12 The word death here means our being separated from EXPERIENCING God's provision, peace, freedom and joy that is ALREADY dwells in us.

Christ's MIND-SET is our effectual WEAPON, and by it we take the TERRORISTS CAPTIVE.

Now we know that the TERRORISTS are in our human MIND – in our deceptive thoughts and beliefs. And our WEAPONS are ALSO NOT of the VISIBLE world. Our true WEAPONS are *divinely powerful* for *pulling down fortresses* of the enemy. II Cor. 10:3-5 Stand firm then, with the belt of truth buckled around your waist, with the breastplate of righteousness in place, and with your feet fitted with the readiness that comes from the gospel of peace. In addition to all this, take up the shield of faith, with which you can extinguish all the flaming arrows of the evil one. Take the helmet of salvation and the sword of the Spirit, which is the word of God. Eph. 6:14-17 NIV

Since our behaviors are fruit of our beliefs, our thoughts and attitudes, we must **ARM OURSELVES** with the **same purpose (MIND-Set) of Christ** and **gird our minds** for action. I Peter 1:13a; I Peter 4:1; Phil. 2:5-8; Col. 3:12; Rom. 8:7 These are the WEAPONS by which we defeat and CAPTURE the TERRORISTS. When we take our thoughts captive to truth, God's *peace will guard our hearts and MINDS* Phil. 4:8 (I know…it still may not fit with our human reasoning that the mind-set of Christ is the way to defeat the enemy!)

Put on the full Armor of God.

But do not be conformed to the world, but be transformed by the RENEWING of the MIND. Rom. 12:2   You are not to walk in the futility of your own MIND Eph. 4:17, but are to Be RENEWED in the spirit of your MIND. Eph. 4:23 by SETTING YOUR MIND on things above (on Truth). Col. 3: 2   The mind set on the flesh is death, but the MIND SET on the SPIRIT is life and peace. Rom. 8:6   (*Remember fleshly ways can look and seem **good***!) **SO gird your MINDS for ACTION as you fix your hope on the Lord's grace.** I Peter 1:13

VIP: We do not take thoughts captive by focusing on putting them away! It won't work. If we do that, we will fail. In order to take our thoughts captive, our focus or mind-set, must be on the Truth. It is much like learning a new language. We must focus on learning the new and not on putting away the existing.

Jesus said, the enemy came to steal, kill and destroy, but He came that you would have life and have it abundantly in the midst of the tribulation. In the world, you WILL have tribulation, but Christ has overcome the world. How? By LOVE. So we are to walk in love in the SAME MANNER as He did to overcome the world. Be on alert because your adversary the devil is seeking who he may devour. We must know the truth so we can discern his deception. It is not by sight nor emotions nor words that we overcome but by exercising faith that expresses itself through LOVE.

That is LOVE in The Present Tense

CHAPTER 26

Fear is Cast Out

Fear is a TERRORIST in our mind.

Often we FEAR rejection. Or we FEAR our needs won't be met. Or we FEAR because we see ourselves as inadequate. We sometimes FEAR what others can do to us…because of their selfishness or hatred or because of their misunderstanding us. We FEAR that our or another's accidents will take away any quality of life we have or desire. What do YOU FEAR?

We are not to fear. Exhortations to God's people to not fear, worry or be anxious are in scripture countless times with urgings such as, "do not fear," "do not be afraid," and "do not be anxious".

Of course, these commands do not contradict the command to "fear God". 1 Peter 2:17 We must be aware that when the Word says for us to **fear God,** it refers to a specific sense of *respect, awe*, and *submission* to God. It is ***reverence*** because of His Power being Love, Light, Grace, Humility, Patience, Wisdom, all Knowing, and because His ways are higher than our ways.

We are told not to fear because God will preserve and protect our soul / mind / heart, and He **prepares His table of good things before** us even *in the presence of our enemies*. He will fight for us. He will justify us to our enemies. He will see that our enemies suffer for their unjust actions toward us. **We are not to fear** what another can do to us. It has been said that fear of being alone without support or connection with another person is the bottom line of all our fears. That would be like the separation mankind had from God as a result of original sin – *before* we were born of His spirit.

A huge reason to CONTINUE in the things we have learned and PRACTICE them is that by this maturing in Him – in Love, FEAR is cast aside!

PERFECT LOVE *casts out* FEAR! "There is **no fear in love. But perfect love drives out fear**, because fear has to do with punishment. The one who fears is not made perfect (maturing) in love" 1 John 4:18

- **"Do not be ANXIOUS about anything,** but in everything, by prayer and petition, with thanksgiving, present your requests to God. **And the peace of God**, which transcends all understanding, **will guard your hearts and your minds** in Christ Jesus". Philippians 4: 6-7

- **"For God has NOT GIVEN us a spirit of FEAR, but of power and of love and of a sound mind"** (NKJV). 2 Timothy 1:7 A spirit of fear and timidity does not come from God. However, sometimes this "spirit of fear" intimidates us, and to overcome it we need to trust God's truth.

- **"Do NOT FEAR**, for I am with you; **Do not ANXIOUSLY look about** you, for I am your God. I will **strengthen** you, surely I will **help** you, Surely I will **uphold you with My righteous right hand."** Isaiah 41:10

- "But even if you should suffer for the sake of righteousness, you are blessed. And do **not FEAR** their intimidation, and **do not be troubled."** 1 Peter 3:14

- "But when they hand you over, **do not WORRY** about how or what you are to say; for **it will be given you in that hour what you are to say**." Matthew 10:19

- "**Blessed is the man who trusts the Lord**, For he will be like a tree planted by the water, That extends its roots by a stream And will not fear when the heat comes; But its leaves will be green, And it **will NOT be ANXIOUS in a year of drought**, nor cease to yield fruit." Jeremiah 17:8

- "So do **NOT WORRY** about tomorrow; for tomorrow will care for itself. Each day has enough trouble of its own." Matthew 6:34

- "…**casting all your ANXIETY** on Him, because He cares for you." 1 Peter 5:7

- "Indeed, the very hairs of your head are all numbered. **Do NOT FEAR**; you are more valuable than many sparrows." Luke 12:7

- "*Listen* to Me, you who know righteousness, A people in whose heart is My law; **Do NOT FEAR the reproach of man**, Nor be dismayed at their revilings (when they mock you, condemn you, curse you, falsely accuse you)." Isaiah 51:7

- "…and he said, "Listen, all Judah and the inhabitants of Jerusalem and King Jehoshaphat: thus says the Lord to you, 'Do **NOT FEAR** or be dismayed **because of this great multitude, for the battle is not yours but God's**." 2 Chronicles 20:15

- "Then your light will break out like the dawn, And your recovery will speedily spring forth; And your righteousness will go before you; The glory of the Lord will be your **rear guard**." Isaiah 58:8

That is LOVE in The Present Tense

CHAPTER 27

Spiritual Sacrifices...
Pleasing to God? Oh, Please.

When we think of

someone being a spiritual sacrifice that usually leads to all kinds to mental images – of someone in a cult, an ascetic hidden in a cave on a mountain, a person in a monastery, or even a religious ceremony in a remote tribe that may sacrifice a human life – all in an effort to "get right with God". These are sacrifices for sin. Of course **our inner sacrifice of LOVE is NOT a sacrifice for sin.** Christ made the sacrifice for sin on our behalf - ***once and for all***. Heb. 10:12

But YES, our **LOVING** others with Christ's mind-set *IS* **SACRIFICIAL**.

Those who have by faith

received God's unconditional Grace, Forgiveness, Acceptance, Love, and indwelling Life *may* have been told that because of His love and our being joined as one with Him forever and because nothing can separate us from His love, that we do NOT need to do anything to PLEASE Him, because we already are pleasing to Him, and *that trying to please God is religious legalism*. NOT SO.

It is true that we are already pleasing to Him.

It is NOT TRUE that we don't need do anything that pleases Him. WHY? Because HE DELIGHTS in our BEING PLEASING to Him and being conformed to His image. Our calling is to GO FURTHER than knowing we are forgiven, knowing what he has done for us, what He has given to us, and our identity in Him. Those things have **EQUIPPED US** to *go further.*

Yes, since we are His own, bought with a price, that is pleasing to God. But after the resurrection, and under the New Covenant of Grace and Love, the believers in the churches are encouraged and exhorted to WALK in a manner WORTHY of their calling and to present themselves as LIVING SACRIFICES. Eph. 4:1; Rom 12:1; 1 Peter 2:5 That would *be proof* to others of their salvation and being Christians. 2 Cor. 8:4, 1 Peter 1:7 We aren't to do this to GET something FROM God, because we ALREADY have been given all things that pertain to Life and Godliness.

> We do it **so that** we will **know Him** and **experience** the fullness of what has ALREADY been given to us - those things of LIFE and GODLINESS within - as we walk in our mortal bodies in this present age. Rom. 8:11 It is true that believers can do nothing to "get closer to God", BUT we can make choices, by His power in us, to allow His life to be revealed through us so that He might be glorified and so that we might more fully KNOW HIM who lives within us. And that is PLEASING to Him.

Knowing this beforehand, we are to BE ON our GUARD so that we are not carried away by the error of unprincipled men and FALL from our own STEADFASTNESS, 2 Peter 3:17 so that we will walk in a MANNER WORTHY of the Lord, to **PLEASE Him** *in all respects,* BEARING FRUIT in every good work and *INCREASING* in the *KNOWLEDGE* of God. Col. 1:10

Paul was speaking to the church at Thessalonica when he said, "we request and exhort you in the Lord Jesus, that as you received from us instruction as to how you ought to walk and PLEASE GOD (just as you actually do walk), that you excel still more. 1 Thess. 4:1 And Paul was definitely NOT talking about religious legalism here! And he says to the Hebrews, "do not neglect DOING GOOD and sharing, for with such **SACRIFICES** God is **PLEASED**. Heb. 13:16 He meant that believers are to do these things - as **everything is to be done - in LOVE.** 1 Cor. 16:13-14 And LOVE is **sacrificial**.

> Thanks be to God, who always leads us to triumph in Christ, and manifests through us the sweet AROMA of the KNOWLEDGE of HIM in every place. 2 Cor. 2:14 But we must be DILIGENT to *SHOW* that we *HAVE BEEN* approved by God. 2 Peter 1:10; 3:14; Heb. 4:11 And *when we KNOW Him, we exude a spiritual aroma to others*.

In our Spirit person, by His doing, we are new creations, holy and righteous saints – priests who are to offer up spiritual sacrifices. "You also, as living stones, are being built up as a spiritual house for a holy priesthood, to offer up SPIRITUAL SACRIFICES acceptable to God through Jesus Christ." 1 Pet. 2:5

Our being LIVING Sacrifices as we serve Him by serving others from the heart, is that fragrant aroma, pleasing to God. **This INNER SACRIFICE is done by our exercising faith that expresses itself by LOVING others.** Again, let it be emphasized that our SACRIFICES to God are NOT for SIN as were the sacrifices of animals under the old obsolete covenant. Because Christ offered up Himself - *ONE SACRIFICE for sins for all time* - and then sat down at the right hand of God. Heb. 10:12

> Our INNER sacrifices of LOVE for others is the sweet aroma of God, and He is PLEASED. This is NOT the same as trying to

do OUTER external fleshly works to try to please God so we will receive something from Him. Even though the fruit of the Spirit which is love, joy, peace, patience, kindness, goodness, faithfulness, gentleness, and self-control appears through us - to a distant observer, a fleshly work of giving all possessions to feed the poor, etc., but WITHOUT LOVE, *may look the same.* So it is all about our LOVING others from the heart with God's love. And when we LOVE others, we KNOW GOD. 1 John. 4:7 With this HE is **PLEASED.** 1 Thess. 2:4

AND as pertaining to morality, believers are urged, by the mercies of God, to present our **bodies** a *living* and *holy* **SACRIFICE**, acceptable to God, which is our spiritual service of WORSHIP. Rom. 12:1 We are to walk in a manner worthy of the Lord, to PLEASE HIM in all respects, bearing fruit in every good work and INCREASING in the KNOWLEDGE OF God. Col 1:10

One can sacrifice without loving. I Corinthins13:3 But one cannot love without sacrificing. Christ's Love is sacrificial. It IS sacrifice. Sacrificial LOVE doesn't seek to have its own way – for its own benefit.

It is costly to go on this path. We have to lose something. We become living sacrifices. Rom.12:1 *Instead of hardening ourselves, fighting back and resisting the hard times, we are to lose or let go of our controls and self-preserving strategies, humbling ourselves and sacrificing our fleshly ways.* This means to be brought low and decrease in importance, instead of trying to be noticed or prove I am right. **This is the mind-set of Christ.**

When we first begin this journey, it may feel like we are disappearing or have no value to anyone. As one of our Grandsons said, "This is serious heart surgery."

For am I now seeking the favor of men, or of God? Or am I striving to please men? If I were still trying to please men, I would not be a *bond-servant* of Christ. Gal. 1:10 **Therefore *be imitators of God,* as beloved children;** and WALK IN LOVE, *JUST AS* CHRIST also LOVED you and GAVE HIMSELF UP FOR US, an offering and a SACRIFICE to God as a fragrant AROMA. Eph. 5:1-2 We must remember that HE sacrificed WHO He was as God as He walked the earth as well as in His death! That represents who GOD **IS** – His very POWER. We are to do the same.

This does *not* mean we are to be *an imitation* in the sense of *being fake*. And this is NOT asceticism where one denies one's self of plea-sures, things, etc. It means to walk by the Spirit. Gal. 5:16 And that is to walk in Love - meaning to walk in *power of His resurrection* and the *fellowship of His sufferings*, being *conformed to His death*, and thus, KNOW HIM *in that way*. Phil. 3:10

And it is when we WALK in His POWER.

That is LOVE in The Present Tense

CHAPTER 28

Not to Follow?
Not to Imitate? Hmmmm...

There has recently been an opinion

that believers who have been born again as new creations in Christ, in union with Him, are to walk by the Spirit - BUT are NOT to "follow Christ" and are NOT to "be imitators of Christ". This view carries the understanding that those phrases mean *to try to copy Christ's outer works or to be fake*, or that the phrases reflect religious legalism.

The phrases mean none of that.

The scriptures below are written for our edification and learning. And these words were spoken by the apostles AFTER Christ's RESURRECTION – under the New Covenant - after He had fulfilled the law for believers and had sent His Spirit to indwell them. New Covenant scriptures exhort others to FOLLOW Christ as well as to follow themselves (the apostles) and to see them as EXAMPLES to *follow in the same manner* in which **they exercised their Faith to Love** others. The apostles spoke to believers, urging them to be IMITATORS of themselves and of God. These scriptures are NOT referring to religious legalism nor copying outer works.

Being IMITATORS of God means that we are to choose to walk by the spirit - His power in us - by putting on Christ's mind-set in our thinking and **exercising His indwelling faith, love and humility in the same LIKENESS and MANNER as Christ did.** And to choose this in the face of suffering and persecution – as He did. For you have been CALLED for this PURPOSE, since Christ also suffered for you, leaving you an example for you to **FOLLOW** in His steps. 1 Peter 2:21 This means to FOLLOW in the same way with the **mind-set of LOVE** – and especially through trials and hard times.

That means to mature in Christ, being conformed in our soul / mind to His image that dwells in our spirit as new creations and to live it out in our relationships. *He is both our identity and our example*. We are told to let this mind be in you that was also in Christ. Phil. 2:5-8 This is when we are destroying speculations and every lofty thing raised up against our knowing God, and we are taking every thought captive to the obedience of Christ. 2 Corinthians 10:5

This has nothing to do with being fake or copying outer works of re-ligious legalism.

> Therefore, be **IMITATORS** of GOD, as beloved children; and **walk in LOVE, just as** Christ also loved you and gave Himself up for us, an offering and a sacrifice to God as a fragrant aroma. Eph. 5:1-2 It is *because* He is Love and our new iden-tity - the new life that dwells in believers - that we can walk in Christ's perfect law of liberty - the law of love – *just as He did*.

We are encouraged to not be sluggish, but **IMITATORS** of those who through FAITH and PATIENCE inherit the promises. Heb. 6:12 Brethren, join in FOLLOWING my example, and observe those who walk according to the pattern you have in us. Phil. 3:17 For you yourselves know how you ought to **FOLLOW** our example, because we did *not* act in an *undisciplined* manner among you - not because we do not have the right to this, but in order to offer ourselves as a model for you, so that you would **FOLLOW** our example. 2 Thess. 3:7,9 Their *inner* **exercising of faith and patience was an example** for the believers to follow!

For you have been called for this purpose, since Christ also s*uffered* for you, leaving you an example for you to **FOLLOW** in His steps. 1 Peter 2:21 Be **IMITATORS** of me, just as I also am of Christ. 1 Cor. 11:1 Therefore I exhort you, be IMITATORS of me. 1 Cor. 4:16 Therefore be **IMITATORS** of God, as beloved children. Eph. 5:1 You also be-came **IMITATORS** of us and of the Lord, having received the word. 1 Thess.1:6 Remember those who led you, who spoke the word of God to you; and considering the result of their conduct, **IMITATE** their **FAITH**. Heb. 13:7 This means our *exercising Faith expressing itself through LOVE in the same manner or likeness as Christ.*

All that has been said is our **PUTTING ON** Christ in our **human mind / soul** by **the renewing of our mind**! There is an old expression, "... Awww, they're just Puttin' on", which means they are being fake.

But this "putting-on" is NOT being an IMITATION or FAKE or copying outer works to gain the favor of men. Gal. 1:10 The night is almost gone, and the day is near. The apostle Paul told new creations in Christ, "Therefore let us lay aside the deeds of darkness and **PUT ON** the armor of light. But **PUT ON** the Lord Jesus Christ, and make no provision for the flesh in regard to *its* lusts." Rom. 13:12,14

For this perishable must **PUT ON** the imperishable, and this mortal must **PUT ON** immortality. We are to PUT ON in our human soul that which ALREADY dwells in us spiritually. But when this perishable will have PUT ON the imperishable, and this mortal will have PUT ON immortality, then will come about the saying that is written, "Death is swallowed up in victory." 1 Cor. 15:53-54 It is when we *walk in victory* in our lives.

PUT ON the **NEW SELF,** which in *the likeness of* God has *(ALREADY)* BEEN CREATED in RIGHTEOUSNESS and HOLINESS of the truth. **PUT ON** the full armor of God, so that you will be able to stand firm against the schemes of the devil. Stand firm therefore, having girded your loins with truth, and having PUT ON the breastplate of righteousness. Eph. 4:24, 6:11,14 But since we are of the day, let us be sober, having PUT ON the breastplate of faith and love, and as a helmet, the hope of salvation. 1 Thess. 5:8

Seeing those truths, let us **PUT ON** the NEW SELF who *is **BEING RENEWED** to a *TRUE KNOWLEDGE* according to *THE IMAGE of the One* (of God) *who created him.* Col. 3:10, Eph. 4:24 So, ***as those who have been chosen of God, holy and beloved, PUT ON a*** heart of compassion, kindness, humility, gentleness and patience; Beyond all these things **PUT ON LOVE**, which is the perfect bond of unity. Col. 3:1,10,12,14 **Putting on the new self** is the same thing as our **pursuing** righteousness /holiness. 1 Tim. 6:10-12; Heb. 12:14-15; 2 Tim.2:22 This is to *walk in* what we already have and *is being* who we already are in Christ..

God's purpose in our walking by the SPIRIT / LOVE in this way is that we will KNOW GOD more completely and in it all, others will see and experience Christ in us and also desire to know God. And HE will be GLORIFIED. 2 Thess. 1:10,12; 1 John 4:7 That is what it means to WALK by the SPIRIT. We are told that if we as new creations in Christ, LIVE by the Spirit, let us *ALSO* WALK by the Spirit. Gal. 5:25

We are to PURSUE these things.

That Is LOVE in The Present Tense

CHAPTER 29

So... What Have You Pursued?

What have you PURSUED?
Longed for? Hoped for? Thirsted for?

Is it Significance? Acceptance? Security? Contentment?

How do you try to quench your thirst? What is your focus? What do you PURSUE? How do you PURSUE what you LONG FOR? By trying to control and "fix" others and circumstances? By trying to please others to avoid rejection? By physical appearance? By distractions like activities, entertainment? Being with people - or on social media? By gossip? By "fun"? By hoopin' and hollarin' ?

Is it by accomplishments, winning, accolades? By being organized? Maybe by pursuing highs in various ways? Perhaps by trying to escape? By desiring power? By travel? By overt or covert control of self or others? By proving you are right? By moving a lot? By being physically fit? By being a minimalist? By STUFF, by money - either spending it on "stuff"- OR by hoarding it?

Sooner or later, we are jaded by it all. And we want more. We can feel entitled. So we try harder doing more of the same. And it isn't working. We can feel let-down, empty – maybe depressed. But we continue to PURSUE whatever we think it takes to be filled – or be fine.

And eventually, OUR PURSUITS can lead to depression, deception, disagreements, controversies and disputes, out of which eventually can come envy, quarrels, abusive language, suspicions, and constant FRICTION. 1 Tim. 6:9, 2 Tim. 2:22-24 And we might feel as if we are plunging into ruin. We ask "WHY?". And there is no lasting peace – no contentment. Even our hopes and dreams might be shattered.

There is nothing wrong with having money, looking nice, being a minimalist, liking sports, having fun, excelling, being right, being responsible, being physically fit, having relationships, etc. But when we look to – PURSUE - these things to bring what we long for - peace, worth, safety, contentment / fulfillment - they don't.

The problem comes when the things we have... HAVE US... have our mind and emotions.

Our strategies / pursuits that seem right can backfire on us. And we can be left tired, depressed, anxious, fearing loneliness or that we don't measure up. Or we are angry because of others' expectations or their violation of our rights. We can take up offenses. Our strategies actually give others or our "things" control over us and make us AS IF we are CAPTIVE to what those others think and do - or to those "things". And then we blame others.

We make excuses, rationalize and tell ourselves it is not what WE are doing that put us in this place of no peace, because our way makes sense to us and maybe it even looks like good work and service to others. But there is no peace...nor joy.

Without realizing it, we are being held captive through philosophy and empty deception, according to the tradition of men, according to the elementary PRINCIPLES of the WORLD. Col 2:8 We wind up holding grudges and bitterness toward others, thinking that if we "let it go and forgive, they won't be held accountable." without realizing that it is destroying US! Do we know that to LOVE is to FORGIVE? I know. It does not make sense to one's HUMAN understanding. But God's way is an enigma, just the opposite, of the fleshly and worldly ways

> What causes *fights and quarrels* among you? Don't they come from your desires that battle within you? You desire but do not have, so you kill. You covet but you cannot get what you want, so you quarrel and fight. You do not have because you do not ask God. When you ask, you don't receive, because you ask with wrong motives, so that you may spend what you get on your pleasures. James 4:1-3 NIV

New creations in Christ are told to flee the evil desires of youth (and immaturity in Christ) and **PURSUE** RIGHTEOUSNESS, FAITH, LOVE and PEACE, along with those who call on the Lord out of *a pure heart*. Don't have anything to do with foolish and stupid arguments, because you know they produce quarrels. And the Lord's **bond-ser-vant** must not be quarrelsome but must be kind to everyone, able to teach, not resentful! 2 Tim. 2:22-24 NIV **We are told to even avoid disputes about religious law because it is useless.** Titus 3:9

What is the REASON for all of our various PURSUITS? Could the bottom line be that we are *really* seeking God's LOVE – His PEACE and fulfillment? And RIGHTEOUSNESS - a conscience that doesn't condemn us, with no fear? But nothing we have tried in this world brings us the PEACE we seek. It is because we are looking in the wrong places.

Do we REALLY want PEACE? Do we *really* want rest, and stillness in our mind, our emotions – in our soul? Do we want to know and

EXPERIENCE God's LOVE, righteousness and forgiveness that we ALREADY have, as we interact in our daily life?

The way the WORLD defines PEACE is the absence of fighting, war and division – outwardly and nationally. But Jesus Christ who IS PEACE, gave Himself to indwell the SPIRIT of believers so we might experience INNER PEACE, Joy and Righteousness while we LIVE IN the world. We as born again believers experience that INNER PEACE in our mind/soul when we stay focused on Truth and choose to walk in it.

So then we are to **PURSUE** the things which **MAKE for inner PEACE** and the BUILDING UP of one another. Rom. 14:19 The things which make for peace are the attributes of LOVE. PURSUE in New Testament Greek - *Dioko* - means to run after, to press on: figuratively of one who in a race runs swiftly to reach the goal. It is to earnestly and eagerly seek after…..PEACE! We are to must seek **peace** and **pursue** it. 1 Peter 3:11

> That WAY of LOVE and inner PEACE is, *at the same time*, a SWORD to the world system! Just as God's LOVE, PEACE, LIFE is a **sweet FRAGRANCE** to **His people,** but **to the world,** it is *at the same time,* the **STENCH of DEATH!** 2 Cor. 2:16 It is amazing that His Truth and Love are POWER and PEACE to some, while the **same thing** is WRATH to others! WHAT another enormous **MYSTERY**!

Jesus said, "My PEACE I leave with you; MY PEACE I give to you; NOT AS the WORLD gives do I give to you. Do not let your heart be troubled, nor let it be fearful. John 14:27 Do you suppose that I came to grant PEACE on EARTH? I tell you, NO, but rather DIVISION; Luke 12:51 "Do not think that I came to bring peace on the earth; I did NOT come to bring peace, but a SWORD. Matt. 10:34 These things I have spoken to you, so that IN ME you may have (inner) PEACE. In the world you have tribulation, but take courage; I have overcome the world."

Christ came in order to shine upon those who sit in darkness and the shadow of death, to guide our feet into **THE WAY** of **PEACE**." Luke 1:79 Actually, we are exhorted to *allow* the PEACE of Christ to RULE in our hearts, to which indeed we were called. Col. 3:15 Wow. *It is our calling*!

Believers are encouraged to live PEACEFUL and QUIET lives, loving others in the face of trails. So others might desire the peace they see in us. We are to relax inwardly, trust His inner provision and protection as WE LOVE others, and His PEACE will guard our hearts and minds! We are to PURSUE experiencing the Life and PEACE that indwells our spirit as believers.

"Whoever would *love life and see good days* must *keep their tongue from evil* and *their lips from deceitful speech*. They *must turn from evil and do good*, they **must SEEK PEACE and PURSUE IT**. 1 Peter 3:10-11 NIV

Whatever our MIND is SET ON, we **PURSUE**. SO we are to be **renewed in the spirit of our minds**. Eph. 4:23 For the **mind set on** the **flesh** (pursues fleshly / worldly things) **is** *death* (our separation from enjoying the blessings that are ours), but the **mind** set on the Spirit is (our delighting in) life and peace. Rom. 8:5-6

We will have the fruit of what we PURSUE / SEEK. And when we *as new creations* in Christ PURSUE / SEEK or have our **MINDS SET** on the **things of the Spirit** within us- *love, joy, peace, patience, kindness, goodness, faithfulness, gentleness, self-control* - we won't worry saying, 'What shall we eat?' or 'What shall we drink?' or 'What shall we wear?' For the pagans run after all these things, and your heavenly Father knows that you need them. When we *pursue / seek first*

His kingdom and His righteousness (that is already ours) all of these things will be given to us (enjoyed by us) as well. Therefore, do not worry about tomorrow, for tomorrow will worry about itself. Each day has enough trouble of its own. Matt. 6: 31-34 NIV

Phil. 4:6-8; Jn. 16:33, 14:27; Rom. 5:1, 8:6-9, 14:17,19; Eph. 2:24; 2 Thess. 3:16; Matt. 10:34. 1 Tim. 2:1-4 (NIV); 1 Thess. 4: 10-12 (NIV) 2 Cor. 2:14-16, Matt. 10:34

Is *Pursuing Righteousness*.... Religious Legalism?

NO. It is NOT religious legalism.

Sometimes people think that striving to do GOOD or RELIGIOUS outer behaviors, will make them acceptable to God or righteous in His sight. But of course that DOESN'T work. Because it isn't true. THAT is Religious Legalism. Believers who are born of God are **ALREADY righteous** in spirit by God's free gift of Forgiveness, Love, Grace, Mercy and Life. They have been equipped to by faith PURSUE RIGHTEOUSNESS. And they are implored to do so!   But WHY?!

We are spirit beings, who have a soul (mind, will and emotions)., and we live in a body. Believers have been born again by God's unconditional Love and Grace. This means they have been given a new spirit that is joined with Christ's spirit. They have been made one spirit with Him. And they are new creations in Christ. They have been made ACCEPTED in Him and RIGHTEOUS by a work of God.

Believers RECEIVE their righteousness BY FAITH, but may not "feel" righteous. Their old FLESHLY programmed thinking in their human mind and the resulting feelings and behaviors may NOT line-up with the truth of WHO they are in their spirit.

We believers can still think and behave in "fleshly" ways that may look outwardly good but backfire on us.... until we MATURE in FAITH by choosing to renew our minds to truth - and then choose by faith to express outwardly who we ALREADY ARE through sacrificial **LOVE** – by the attitude of a servant, humility, preferring others above ourselves, godliness, gentleness, peace. **THAT is when we PURSUE** the RIGHTEOUSNESS that ALREADY indwells us. This PURSUING is our WORK of FAITH that requires our perseverance. Sometimes it can be like a fight. We are exhorted to "fight the good FIGHT of FAITH" – especially when facing adversity or others betraying or crucifying us.

But you, **MAN OF GOD**, flee from all this (worldly lusts), and **PURSUE righteousness, godliness, faith, love, endurance and gentleness.** Fight the good fight of the faith. TAKE HOLD of the eternal life to which you were called (and which is ALREADY in you.) 1 Tim. 6:10-12   This is when we **pursue peace** with all people, and the **holiness** without which no one will see the Lord. It is when we leave bitterness and quarrels behind. Heb. 12:14-15

Who knew that believers who **are holy** in spirit are to **pursue holiness!**

Pursuing holiness is living out our faith by LOVE and is likened to a race we run. Heb.12:1; 1 Cor. 9:24   And we may fail on the way, but we re-focus on the GOAL. The GOAL is to LOVE others, and in BY THIS to *experientially* KNOW God and His RIGHTEOUSNESS more completely. (This is not just to know facts about Him and about who we are as new creations).

We are told to flee from immature lusts and PURSUE RIGHTEOUSNESS, faith, love *and* peace, with those who call on the Lord from a pure heart. 2 Tim. 2:22   Therefore do NOT LET SIN reign in your MORTAL BODY so that you obey its lusts, and do not go on presenting the members of your body to sin as instruments of unrighteousness; but PRESENT YOURSELVES to God as those alive from the dead, and your members as INSTRUMENTS of RIGHTEOUSNESS to God. Rom. 6: 6-13

This speaks of these things happening in this PRESENT AGE. For the grace of God has appeared, bringing salvation to all men, instructing us to deny ungodliness and worldly desires and to live sensibly, righteously and godly in the PRESENT AGE. Titus 2:11-12   He gave Himself for our sins so that He might RESCUE US FROM this PRESENT EVIL AGE, according to the will of our God and Father. Gal.1:4

As we focus on PURSUING Righteousness and Peace, as a result, we leave things of the flesh and the world behind.

We ABANDON them.

That is LOVE in the Present Tense

CHAPTER **30**

Mysteries of the Abandoned

The episodes show empty buildings,

desolate bridges, fortresses and tunnels, etc. that have been left behind. They were ineffective, and the energy, productivity and focus had been placed somewhere else.

Often our energy and focus is on clinging to our productivity, to memorabilia, finances, to other people and even to our addictions to escape and to avoid feeling desolate, anxious, and maybe ashamed. But the more we try to fill emptiness in these ways, the more hollow and anxious we can feel. We may think something is wrong with us. Our ways backfire on us, and we blame and rationalize. We seek life and peace by these strategies and we can't find it. We don't realize that our destructive emotions and behaviors are a result of our own beliefs and resulting ways.

The truth is that our old ineffective beliefs and behaviors that are called, *flesh*, must be abandoned. They do not represent the Truth of who we are in Christ nor how we are to enjoy peace, security and fulfillment. However as with those old desolate edifices of the past, *the focus was not on leaving them behind. **It was on new pursuits.***

Likewise, our mind can't be set on putting the old things away, because that doesn't work.

The inner life, peace and security believers seek comes as we choose by faith to FOCUS ON and PURSUE learning a new and living way of Spirit and Truth. Our mind is to be set on a continual awareness of the truth of one's inner union with Christ, His sufficiency for us, and our living out His mind-set. We will then begin to experience His life and peace. Anxiety, loneliness and fear will be left behind – ABANDONED.

As was presented in a former chapter, that is how our old deceitful desires, fleshly beliefs and the resulting emotions and behaviors are *PUT OFF*. Eph. 4:22,25 NIV When we *continue* in this way, the peace of God, which surpasses all comprehension, will guard our hearts and minds in Christ Jesus. Phil. 4:7

There are believers who *mentally* know their identity in Christ as new creations, and yet often still live with SHAME and FEAR because of their past sins and other's opinions. When our FOCUS is on past failures and on other's opinions, **instead of** our MIND being SET on Christ's Life in us, on His forgiveness, on His having abolished death on our behalf, on His total sufficiency for us, on our crucifixion with Him in the spiritual realm and on LOVING others, we CONDEMN OURSELVES – our **own** conscience! We are NOT to do that, because God does not condemn us who are in Christ! Rom. 8:1 He was crucified so that we would have a conscience FREE from condemnation - GUILT, SHAME and FEAR.

To *abide* means to *continue* and believers have been equipped not only to, by faith believe, but to also to GROW up – to CONTINUE IN Christ – to persevere in exercising faith and belief of the truth, forgiving ourselves, accepting ourselves as who we are as new creations, and trusting Christ as our protection from the world – as we LOVE others. This is our PURSUIT of holiness. We can't focus on our former sins, fears, rejections by others, and the resulting emotions IF our human mind is SET ON things above – and on the truth of RECEIVING and GIVING LOVE!

That is when our fleshly ways – our false beliefs, damaging emotions and behaviors, shame and fears - are ABANDONED.

Now, little children, abide (continue and press on) in Him, so that when He appears, we may have confidence and not shrink away from Him in SHAME at His coming. 1 John 2:28   As one's **focus is on *receiving* and *giving* God's love**, our *fleshly strategies* with any resulting *SHAME* and *FEAR* are being ABANDONED. When we continue and press on in FAITH expressing itself through LOVE (Gal. 5:6) even in the middle of hard times, those former things in our human mind and emotions grow dim and are LEFT BEHIND. This persevering in FAITH is to bring God's LOVE - His life – to light the world through us, so that He will be glorified. It is a believer's very calling.

Have you thought about what you would be *abandoning* if you focused on walking with your faith expressing itself by Love?

When our own fleshly ways ARE ABANDONED, it is when we **enter into** (experience) **God's REST** – His Peace that is ALREADY ours. For the one who has entered His rest has himself also **rested** (ceased KJV) **from** his **works**, as God did from His. Heb. 4:10

Heb. 10:22; Gal. 5:4; 1 John 2:28; Gal. 5:6; 2 Tim. 1:10

That is LOVE in The Present Tense

CHAPTER 31

What Does REST Mean?

Sometimes we hear,

"Just REST in the Lord and He will live through you".

But – what does that MEAN? Is that Truth? The terms, "rest in the Lord", "rest in Christ" and "rest in Him" are **NOT IN** the New Testament. WHAAATT?

There remains a Sabbath **REST** for the people of God. For the one who has entered His REST has himself also *rested (ceased KJV) from* his works, as God did from His. Therefore let us **BE DILIGENT** to ENTER that REST, so that no one will fall, through following the same ex-ample of disobedience (of walking after the flesh). Heb. 4:9-11

"REST" in the Greek in this context **means *inner repose, relaxation, peace*.** And the word **"PEACE"** in the Greek can convey the same sense of *INNER REST, well-being, serenity and harmony,*

So the word, "REST" in the above scriptures means God's PEACE. The phrase, "RESTING from his works", means CEASING from one's "works" of living /striving after the flesh to make life work the best way he/she knows how. Remember these works of the flesh can look right or be religious - or look evil. Both are disobedience. And ceasing from one's fleshly works happens as a SIDE-EFFECT of focusing on, and walking by, the Spirit and Truth. Gal. 5:16 This focusing on walking in LOVE by the spirit is an inner choice to persevere in faith especially in the face of rejections and hard times. So REST does not mean we don't persevere and pursue righteousness and press on in faith.

When we endure in Faith, walking by the Spirit and Truth to LOVE others, we enter into - **experience in our SOUL** – the REST/ PEACE that ALREADY dwells in our spirit as believers. Focusing on and walking by the Spirit is *not passivity*. It is CHOOSING, by faith, to be inwardly diligent, steadfast, persevering in truth – even when circumstances are hard, unfair and painful. It is to ABIDE. And to abide, rather than meaning passivity, means TO CONTINUE in those ways.

> We have to be intentional – PRESSING ON and continuing in faith by the power of Christ indwelling Spirit. As we persevere, we will ENTER into (experience or lay hold on) His REST / PEACE – that eternal life within us. And as has been stated many times, we ACCESS by faith that grace in which we (already) stand! (Rom. 5:2) Paul said, "......but I PRESS ON so that I may LAY HOLD OF that for which also I was laid hold of by Christ Jesus." (Phil 3:12)   The mind set on the Spirit is life and peace. Romans 8:6   **It is PEACE / REST to our SOUL.**

Again one might ask, "WELL.. What does having one's mind set on the Spirit and walking by the Spirit look like? What does that MEAN?"

Yet another way of verbalizing the SAME THING was when Jesus said in reference to the New Covenant, "TAKE MY **YOKE** upon you and learn from Me, for I am GENTLE AND HUMBLE in heart, and you will find **REST for your SOULS.**" Matthew 11:29 A yoke is a restraint. And **Christ's restraint is LOVE** which is SACRIFICIAL and it is

INTENTIONAL. The *YOKE we are to take is to LOVE one another*. Here, as in the Luke 13:24 reference, Christ was speaking in meta- phor of the *rest / peace* of the Kingdom of God that was to be made manifest and experienced for believers after His resurrection.

In other words, when we are **diligent** and **persevere in taking His yoke** upon ourselves, it is the way for our SOUL to experience REST - the Joy, Peace and Righteousness that dwells in our new SPIRIT. We are to take THIS yoke and "keep standing firm and do not be subject again to a yoke of slavery" (to the flesh OR religious law) Gal. 5:1

This is when OTHERS see and experience CHRIST IN and THROUGH us. Believers are the ones who have been made adequate to be ser- vants of the New Covenant. 2 Cor. 3:6 Being servants of the New Covenant is being diligent to exercise faith that expresses itself by LOVE. Gal. 5:6

But to LOVE can feel SO hard when we feel BETRAYED and DISAPPOINTED.

Apart from all of the things that are going on in our country, at times in life most of us can be wronged, betrayed and / or disappointed by friend or family, regardless of the other's intent. As a result, hurt, loneliness and grief can overwhelm us. Then anger can come. And depression. Sometimes we fight back. We might make excuses. We can criticize them and their decisions / actions. We put them down. We shut them off. We can even accuse them of destroying the rela- tionship. We don't realize that we are doing the same thing that we accused them of doing.

The only answer to the pain, grief and anger is to respond with the mind-set / attitude of Christ. With His **YOKE** of **LOVE**. And that is to humble one's self, take the form of a servant, preferring the other above one's self. It is to forgive, to be gentle, kind, patient, helpful, and giving of one's self. This is our taking His YOKE. A yoke is a re-straint. *And we are to choose it.*

Christ's YOKE *is* LOVE. And it isn't "touchy/feely" love. It will usu-ally go against one's f*eelings*. It is often a hard choice to make. BUT it is a choice believers are adequate to make. It is what we are called to do as believers. It may *feel* scary, embarrassing or *feel* shameful to apologize for our negative responses to them and look wrong – even if we believe we were right.   Sometimes, in order to LOVE, we will need to let go of our fleshly self-protections and that can *feel* scary. But Christ's yoke of LOVE is a yoke of freedom and rest.

In order to enjoy that freedom, peace and joy - His REST in our SOUL - which we might experience gradually, we must take His YOKE, while KNOWING it is the right thing to do. The relationship may or may not be restored. But it might be – and be better than before.

The one who chooses this way will walk free from anger, from self-condemnation, from fear - and will have joy and peace that is be-yond human understanding - **enjoying REST for the Soul**.   Matt. 11:29 And yes. It is opposite the world's way of dealing with things. But it is God's way. God IS love.

God's PEACE / REST:

These things I have spoken to you so that in Me you may **have peace**. In the world you have tribulation, but take courage; I have overcome the world." John 16:33

Let the peace of Christ, to which you were indeed called in one body, **rule** in your hearts; and be thankful. Col.. 3:15

There is glory, honor, and **peace** to everyone who does what is good, Rom. 2:10

For the mind set on the flesh is death, but the **mind set on the Spirit** is **life** and **peace**, Rom. 8:6

For the kingdom of God is not eating and drinking, but righteousness and **peace** and joy in the Holy Spirit. Rom. 14:17

So then we **pursue** the things which make for **peace** and the building up of one another. Rom. 14:19

Now may the God of hope fill you with all joy and **peace** in believing, so that you will abound in hope by the power of the Holy Spirit. Rom. 15:13

For **He Himself is our peace**, Ep. 2:14

These things I have spoken to you so that in Me you may have **peace**. In the world you have tribulation, but take courage; I have overcome the world. John 16:33

Do not be anxious about anything, but in everything by prayer and pleading with thanksgiving let your requests be made known to God. And the **peace of God**, which surpasses all comprehension, will guard your hearts and minds in Christ Jesus. Phil. 4:6-7

Now may the **Lord of peace** Himself continually grant you **peace** in every circumstance. 2 Thess. 3:16

That is LOVE in The Present Tense

CHAPTER 32

Now, What IS it…to Worship?

Some who *know their identity* in Christ,

their *security* and *sufficiency* in Him, say that since they are eternally secure spiritually, "there is nothing wrong with having fun." There are those who believe this, and they often struggle with various emotional and physical hindrances of some kind, or maybe even addictions. They rationalize and see nothing wrong with it, because God still loves them. Some may lead *worship music* at their church gatherings and love the momentary *feeling* of it all. But they are defeated and don't understand that they are blocking their experience of God's Life and Peace that is already theirs.

Well then, what is WORSHIP?

But a time is coming, and even now has arrived, when the true **worshipers** will **worship** the Father in **spirit** and **truth**; for such people the Father seeks *to be* His **worshipers**. God is **spirit**, and those who **worship** Him must **worship** in **spirit** and **truth**." John 4:23-24

Have they been taught that our choosing to sacrificially LOVE others - to walk in Godliness with the mind-set of Christ as in Phil. 2:5-8 and Eph. 5:2 – IS our **worshiping** God in Spirit and Truth? John 4:24

In addition, believers are urged, in view of God's mercy, to offer our BODIES as a LIVING sacrifice, HOLY and PLEASING to GOD - (because) this is our **true** and **proper worship**. Rom. 12:1 NIV 'Wow. Who knew that is WORSHIP?

So, "to worship" means to, in reverence, serve others by LOVE and humility from the heart.

This is NOT asceticism nor denying one's self things nor having an *appearance* of wisdom, with a self-imposed worship, a *false humility* and a *harsh treatment of the body*, as these things lack any value in *restraining sensual indulgence*. Col. 2:23

Believers / saints who have been made adequate by the power of the Spirit within them, need to know that **immorality** or any **impurity** or **greed** must not even be named among them, as is proper among saints. Eph. 5:3 Therefore *consider* the members of your earthly body as **dead to** immorality, impurity, passion, evil desire, and greed, which amounts to idolatry. Col. 3:5 Yes, regardless of what you might *feel*.

> For this is the will of God, your sanctification that is, that you abstain from sexual *immorality*. 1 Thess. 4:3 NIV Yes, believers already ARE sanctified **spiritually**, but our sanctification is not *appropriated **in our soul*** and **body** at our new birth as our spirit is.

> So we must grow in our *experience* of it. To be *sanctified* means to be "set apart" and dedicated for God's use, and as we by faith walk AS who we ALREADY are in Christ, this is our *appropriating* our sanctification. The verb, *to appropriate*, here means to "take possession of" what is ours. **And it is our spiritual service of WORSHIP**. Rom. 12:1

Everyone who names the name of the Lord is to abstain from evil *desires* of all kinds. Now in a large house there are not only gold and silver vessels, but also vessels of wood and of earthenware, and some to honor and some to dishonor. Therefore, **if anyone cleanses himself from these things**, he will be a *vessel for honor*, sanctified, useful to the Master, **prepared for every good work.** Pursuing *righteousness, faith, love and peace,* with those who call on the Lord from a pure heart 2 Tim. 2:19-22 These are the **good works** (of FAITH working through LOVE) *that we are created for.* We are to **abstain from** every form of evil. Now may the God of peace Himself sanctify you entirely; and may your **spirit** and **soul** and **body** be preserved complete, without blame at the coming of our Lord Jesus Christ. 1 Thess. 5:22-24

Since we know that, we are to make every effort to add to our faith goodness; and to goodness, knowledge; and to knowledge, self-control; and to self-control, perseverance; and to perseverance, godliness; and to godliness, mutual affection; and to mutual affection, love. For **if you possess these qualities *in increasing measure*, they will keep you from being *ineffective* and *unproductive in your KNOWLEDGE of* our *Lord Jesus Christ*.** 2 Peter 1:5-8 NIV

Our WORSHIP is also to Love by BUILDING each other.... UP

Are we believers being taught to not be critical or take up offenses, not to be jealous or arrogant, but to forgive? Are we being encouraged to not do anything from selfishness or by drawing attention to ourselves in any way, but to, WITH HUMILITY of MIND, regard one another as more important than ourselves? Phil. 2:3

We are to know that each of us as believers in the body of Christ have been given talents and gifts to help equip each other and BUILD each other UP - SO THAT we may be united in our faith and MATURE in

KNOWING HIM more completely – in His FULLNESS. Eph. 4:11-13 That is to be our FOCUS.

When all members of the body of Christ work together in a suitable way, it is to help each other grow in building itself up in LOVE. So BUILD up one another – ENCOURAGE others by LOVING them! Eph. 4:16; 1 Thess. 5:1,13   YES…and that also means we are to DO THE SAME with those who are religious legalists. They need to SEE the FULLNESS and LOVE of GOD in this way rather than by trying to convince them by arguments and debates about words / doctrines – which only lead to quarrels, controversial questions and disputes about words, out of which arise suspicions and constant friction. 1 Tim 6:3-5

So then pursue the things which make for peace and the **building up** of **one another**. Rom. 14:9 Therefore, encourage **one another** and **build one another up**, just as you also are doing. 1 Thess. 5:11

Our very purpose as we LOVE is to show truth to the poor, proclaim release to the captives, recovery of spiritual sight to the blind, and set free those who are inwardly oppressed. It is to bring good news to the afflicted, bind up the brokenhearted, proclaim liberty to captives, and freedom to those who are imprisoned in their heart and conscience.

We are to comfort those who mourn - giving them a garland instead of ashes, the oil of gladness instead of mourning, the mantle of praise instead of a spirit of heaviness. So we will be called and seen by others as oaks of righteousness.   Our focus and intent is to BE who we ARE as the planting of the LORD, so that He may be glorified Luke 4:18; Isaiah 61

Therefore encourage one another and build up one another, just as you also are doing. 1 Thess. 5:11 Our purpose is to let others see and experience Truth revealed through us and to share the Truth of the Law of the Spirit of Life in Christ. The LAW of LOVE.

Above all, keep *FERVENT* IN YOUR LOVE for one another, because love covers a multitude of sins. Be hospitable to one another without complaint. As each one has received a *special* gift, employ it in serving one another as good stewards of the manifold grace of God. Whoever speaks, *is to do so* as one who is speaking the words of God; whoever serves *is to do so* as one who is SERVING by the STRENGTH which GOD SUPPLIES; so that in all things God may be glorified through Jesus Christ, to whom belongs the glory and dominion forever and ever. Amen. 1 Peter 4:8-11

When we continue in serving and loving others by His LOVE, it is when others see His Life in and through us and it is when Christ, who is our life, **is revealed**. Col. 3:4 It is when His glory is revealed. It is when He is glorified!

Scriptures using the words "Love One Another and "Love Each Other":

John 13:34-35, 15:12,17; Rom. 13:8; 1 Thess. 4:9; 1 Peter 3:8,4:8; 1 John 3:11, 23; 4:7, 11-12 ; 2 John 5

To WORSHIP is to walk by the Spirit which IS to walk in LOVE

In summary, we have seen that the Old **Covenant Law is** fulfilled in **ONE word – LOVE.** Gal. 5:14**;** Rom. 13:8 The requirement of the Law (LOVE) might be fulfilled in us who do not walk according to the flesh but according to **the Spirit**. Rom. 8:4

We have seen that the mind of Christ **is LOVE** itself. **SO walking according to the Spirit within us is to LOVE with our human mind-set being the same as Christ's!** Love is the fruit of the Spirit.

If we live by the Spirit, let us also *walk by the Spirit*. The fruit of the Spirit is love, joy, peace, patience, kindness, goodness, faithfulness, gentleness, self-control; against such things there is no law. Gal. 5:22-23

Walk in love, *just as* Christ also **loved** you and gave Himself up for us, an *offering and a sacrifice to God* as a fragrant aroma. Eph. 5:2

Since **walking according to the spirit** *IS to* LOVE, then walking according to the Spirit is being *PATIENT, KIND (humble) and* is *not jealous*; does *not brag and* is *not arrogant, not act unbecomingly*; *not seek its own*, is *not provoked*, does *not take into account a wrong suffered*, *does not rejoice in unrighteousness*, but *rejoices with the truth*; *bears* all things, *believes* all things, *hopes* all things, *endures* all things. Love never fails. 1 Cor. 13:3-8.

"Now for this very reason also, **applying** all **diligence in your faith,** supply moral excellence, and in *your* moral excellence, knowledge, and in *your* knowledge, self-control, and in *your* self-control, perseverance, and in *your* perseverance, godliness, and in *your* godliness, brotherly kindness, and in *your* brotherly kindness, LOVE." 2 Peter 1:5-7

So be on your guard; stand firm in the faith; be courageous; be strong. Do EVERYTHING in LOVE. 1 Cor. 16:13-14

As believers, we have learned of God's love and goodness toward us – His indwelling life, His Power, Protection and Provision. We praise Him for that. We have faith and pray, asking Him for the good things He gives. Our focus often is on His meeting our needs and desires – on *what we receive* from Him.

We may know He supplies all of our needs, but **we are to go further** and **mature in love** with our minds set on our **knowing God** more intimately – which is to have our focus on being conformed to His image of loving and giving up ourselves for others. We are exhorted to **abide in love** – meaning we are to **continue** in receiving God's Love and pressing on in our faith being expressed by loving others. When we **love**, we know we have passed from death into life. 1 John 3:14

> When we LOVE sacrificially is when we know God, glorify Him, praise and honor Him. It is when we WORSHIP Him.

Eph. 5:2 – "... walk in **love**, just as Christ also loved you and gave Himself up for us, an offering and a sacrifice to God as a fragrant aroma.

John 15: 17 - This is my commandment, that you **love** one another.

Rom. 13:10 - **Love** is the fulfillment of *the* law.

I Cor.16:14 - Let all that you do be done in **love.**

Gal. 5:14 - For the whole Law is fulfilled in one word, in the *statement*, "You shall **love** your neighbor as yourself."

I John 3:14 - We **know** that we have **passed out of death into life**, because we **love** the brethren. He who does **not love** abides **in death.**

Matt. 22:37- 40 - And He said to him, "'You shall **love** the Lord your God with all your heart, and with all your soul, and with all your mind [38] This is the great and [b]foremost commandment. [39] The second is like it, " You shall **love** your neighbor as yourself"' [40] On these two commandments depend the whole Law and the Prophets."

John 13:34 - A new commandment I give to you, that you **love** one another, even as I have loved you, that you also love one another.

I John 4:8 - The one who does not love does not know God, for God is **love.**

I John 4:12 - No one has seen God at any time; if we **love** one another, God abides in us, and His **love** is perfected *(made mature)* in us. *Italics mine.*

I John 4:16 - God is love, and the one who **abides in love** abides in God, and God abides in him.

John 13:35 - By this all men will know that you are My disciples, if you have **love** for one another."

John 15:9 - Just as the Father has **love**d Me, I have also **love**d you; **abide in My love**.

1 John 4:7 - Beloved, let us love one another, for **love** is **from God**; and everyone **who loves is born of God and knows God.**

1 Cor. 16:13-14 Be on your guard; stand firm in the faith; be courageous; be strong. **do everything in love.**

We have now seen that our *true WORSHIP is expressing our LOVE for* God BY our Loving others with His kind OF LOVE. God's **will, purpose and intention for us** is that we, by faith and the power of His Spirit in us, LOVE others and give ourselves up for them as Christ gave Himself up for us. Eph. 5:2 This is God's LOVE. And it is all that counts Gal. 5:6. This is to worship Him in Spirit and in Truth. Jn. 4:23-24 This is when we KNOW HIM as He knows us. 1 Jn. 4:7 And our KNOWING GOD is ETERNAL LIFE Jn. 17:3.

Jesus said He came **to serve, not to be served.** Now think about it. This **ATTITUDE of LOVE** is the Spirit and mind-set of the CREATOR and master OF ALL THINGS. Now **THAT is** *Power.*

What a paradox to earthly thinking!

But an hour is coming, and **NOW IS**, when the true worshipers will worship the Father in spirit and truth; for such people the Father seeks to be His worshipers. God is spirit, and those who worship Him must WORSHIP in SPIRIT and TRUTH." John 4:23-24   Since **God is Love**, to worship Him means our LOVING others. The one who does not love does not know God, for God IS LOVE. 1 John 4:8

We know we are a new creation worshipping God walking in LOVE according to the Spirit:

- when **we do not** (merely) **LOVE with words or speech but we LOVE with actions and in truth**. This is how we know that we belong to the truth and how we set our hearts at rest in his presence. 1 John 3:18-20

- when we **love** one another, for **love** comes from **God.** Everyone who **love**s has been born of **God** and **know**s **God.** 1 John 4:7 Whoever follows His word, in him the **love** of **God** has truly been perfected. By this (LOVE) we **know** that we are in Him 1 John 2:5

- when we who live are constantly being delivered over to death for Jesus' sake, so that **the life of Jesus also may be manifested** *(revealed)* **in our mortal flesh.** 2 Cor. 4:11

- when **Christ, who is our life, is revealed,** then you also will be **revealed with Him in glory.** Col. 3:4

- when we are **growing** and **being conformed** to Christ's image, His likeness. Phil. 3:10

- when our hearts/minds are **being established in holiness.** I Thess. 3:13

- when **we bear fruit** (of the spirit) to God. Rom. 7:4; Gal. 5:22

- when out of our innermost being **will flow rivers of living water**.'" John 7:38

That is LOVE in the Present Tense

Following is a visual illustration of a New Creation when we LOVE. It is when we are being conformed Christ's image in our SOUL and His Life is being revealed through us. It is our Worship.

Christ's Life Being Revealed In and Through Us

The diagram below might be a helpful aid in understanding the truth of how our **reliance on our FLESHLY way (the gray areas) is being broken away and abandoned - by the renewing of our mind to Christ's mind-set** and **His response of LOVE - to the Hard Times of daily life**. By this response, Christ's Life and the Fruit of the Spirit flow out to be EXPRESSED and EXPERIENCED BY us and THROUGH us so others will see Christ in us.

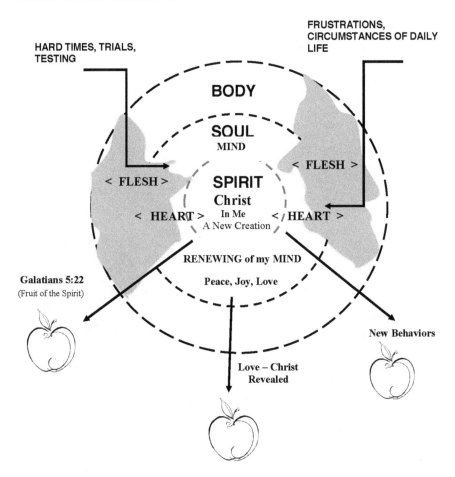

CHAPTER 33

ABIDE = Remain / Continue in These Things

As we conclude

these pages on LOVE and walking after the Spirit, we must remember this occurs as we actively choose to **set our mind on the Spirit and Truth** in our daily circumstances and REMAIN in this. This is **to ABIDE in Christ.** *It is not a life of inner passivity as one might suppose.*

> The definition of ABIDE or REMAIN means *to intentionally* CONTINUE to grow in the experience of our union with Christ. It involves our attitudes and decisions. It *results* in our *enjoying* our Life in Him.

Jesus speaking of the New Covenant to come after the resurrection said, "**Remain in Me**, and I in you. Just as the branch cannot bear fruit of itself but **must remain in** the vine, so neither *can* you unless you **remain in Me**. I am the vine, you are the branches; the one who remains in Me, and I in him **bears much fruit**, for apart from Me you can do nothing." John 15:4-5

There are several words for *abide* in the Greek. But the root from which all the other verbs come is *meno* which is defined as meaning "intensive." When we abide in something, we remian loyal to it even unto death. When we abide, we **remain** in a certain place even when the rest of the world has left us behind. To abide means to **continue** in whatever is being done even when it is hard and the urge to quit is almost too much. The word **abide** means to cling to something and have faith in it, even when it seems to have failed. It means to **endure**, to **persevere,** to **press on**, to **stand firm,** to **remain**.

In **order to ABIDE**, we *discipline our hearts and minds to press on and stand firm* in the truths presented in this book. ABIDING is our CONTINUING in: our *obedience of exercising faith that expresses itself through love.* It's all that matters.

I am giving you a **new commandment**, that you love one another; just as I have loved you, that you also love one another. John 13:34 **LOVE** is *the identifying mark of who you are*..... and of Christianity itself.

Our ABIDING in Christ RESULTS in His Life and mind-set in us appearing outwardly - His nature of humility and Love being revealed through us - our BEARING THE FRUIT OF HIS SPIRIT which is love, kindness, patience, joy, goodness, gentleness, peace, faithfulness, self-control. Gal. 5:22 So don't receive the grace of God in vain. 2 Corinthians 6:1 But *continue* in it.

"...yet He has now reconciled you in His fleshly body through death, in order to present you before Him holy and blameless and beyond reproach—if indeed you **continue in the faith** firmly established and *steadfast,* and *not moved away from the hope of the gospel* that you have heard..."   Colossians 1:22-23

The goal of this book has been to present mysteries that were revealed and brought to light by the gospel. 2 Tim. 1:10 This included many different ways of explaining the SAME THING - the ONE thing - of walking in LOVE from a pure heart and a good conscience and a sincere faith.1 Tim. 1:5

A believer's life is to *be lived by loving others* **just as Christ LOVED us by serving, preferring others above Himself and giving Himself up for us.** It is to humble one's self to be a servant even through difficult times and even persecution which is just the opposite of what the world believes a conqueror to be. The result is Christ's Life being revealed through us for others to experience. The result is one knowing God intimately. The result is that we walk in the fullness of inner freedom, peace and joy that is ours in Christ.

That is LOVE in the Present Tense